TO ROTH
OR
NOT TO ROTH

The Guide to Tax Planning in Retirement

By Billy Voyles

This book discusses general concepts for retirement income planning and is not intended to provide tax or legal advice. Individuals are urged to consult with their tax and legal professionals regarding these issues.

The stories and characters in this book are fictional. Each story combines facts and circumstances redacted to highlight the subject matter of each chapter. Facts and circumstances are fictional and do not represent any one client in part or whole. They are included as an educational tool. No story should be treated to apply to the reader's individual circumstances. Always consult with your tax professional, attorney, and advisor before taking any action.

Investment advisory services are offered through Foundations Investment Advisors, LLC ("Foundations"), an SEC registered investment adviser. The content provided is intended for informational and educational purposes only. Additionally, the information contained herein does not constitute an offer to sell any securities or represent an express or implied opinion or endorsement of any specific investment opportunity, offering or issuer. Each individual investor's situation is different, and any ideas provided may not be appropriate for your particular circumstances. Foundations deems reliable any statistical data or information obtained from or prepared by third party sources cited throughout, but in no way guarantees its accuracy or completeness. The primary goal in converting retirement assets into a Roth IRA is to reduce the future tax liability on the distributions you take in retirement, or on the distributions of your beneficiaries. The information provided is to help you determine whether or not a Roth IRA conversion may be appropriate for your particular circumstances. Please review your retirement savings, tax, and legacy planning strategies with your legal/tax advisor to be sure a Roth IRA conversion fits into your planning strategies. All Rights Reserved.

Any comments regarding safe and secure investments and guaranteed income streams refer only to fixed insurance products. They do not in any way refer to investment advisory products. Rates and guarantees provided by insurance products and annuities are subject to the financial strength of the issuing insurance company; not guaranteed by any bank or the FDIC.

Copyright © 2024 by Magellan Financial and Billy Voyles. All rights reserved. No part of this publication may be reproduced, distributed, or transmitted in any form or by any means, electronic or mechanical, including photocopying, recording, or by any information storage and retrieval system, without written permission of the publisher, except in the case of brief quotations embodied in critical reviews and certain other noncommercial uses permitted by copyright law.

Printed in the United States of America

First Printing, 2024

Cover and interior design by the Magellan Creative Team.

TABLE OF CONTENTS

INTRODUCTION 1

CHAPTER 1
    THE BIG SHIFT 7

CHAPTER 2
    INCOME 19

CHAPTER 3
    TAXES IN RETIREMENT 35

CHAPTER 4: ROTH IRA CONVERSIONS
    SEED OR HARVEST? 47

CHAPTER 5: SECTION 7702 LIFE INSURANCE
    LIFE INSURANCE FOR THE LIVING 65

CHAPTER 6: FINAL THOUGHTS
    ROTH OR NO? 87

GLOSSARY OF TERMS 91

INTRODUCTION

On June 2nd, 2023, Congress agreed to suspend the debt ceiling restriction which was set at $31.4 trillion dollars. As of this writing in October of 2023, the National debt had increased to $33.5 trillion—over $2.1 trillion dollars of debt added in just 4 months. That's $500 billion dollars per month, and over $16 billion per day.

We toss around these numbers as if they no longer matter and there's an infinite amount of resources to tackle such mountains of debt; but let's take a look at exactly how big one trillion really is.

How long does it take to count a million seconds? Eleven days, 13 hours, 46 minutes, and 40 seconds. Okay, so how long would it take to count to a billion? We will round off here, but it would be about 33 years! Counting to a trillion? That would take you over 33 thousand years.

Why are we counting to a trillion? The U.S. national debt is at $33 trillion and rising, millions of Americans are preparing to retire with tax-deferred accounts like 401(k)s and IRAs, and a perfect tax storm is brewing.

In other words, tax planning in retirement isn't just important—it is more important than ever. That wasn't always the case, but the times have changed. Many Americans used to have pensions and an amount from Social Security that covered their living expenses. They didn't need to have much or any money in the market. Today, defined contribution plans like 401(k)s have replaced most pensions—and traditional 401(k)s come with a big tax bill once they are withdrawn for income.

There is a storm brewing, but the good news is that we know it is coming and we can prepare for it. During your working years when you are earning, saving, and investing, dollar cost averaging is on your side. You can enjoy a lower annual tax bill while you put pre-tax dollars in your 401(k). But after you retire and you start reversing the flow by taking money out of your accounts, you are at the mercy of whatever tax rate and tax bracket you fall under. Instead of just filing your taxes each year, now is the time to plan ahead so you can maximize the net amount you get to keep in your pocket.

I like to explain tax planning by comparing it to getting ready for a road trip. Hitting the open road is one of life's most exciting pleasures. But even the whim and spontaneity of a road trip requires some planning. You need a car, some gas, a destination, food to eat, places to sleep. And you need a map or a GPS. You need to see where you are and where you are going. It might feel like you are just jumping in the car, but there is more to it than that. You can't just jump into retirement, either, and expect to get where you hope to go. You will need an income, insurance, and a strategy that will protect your money so it lasts as long as you do.

What could threaten your money? **Inflation**, health care costs, market **volatility**—there are a whole host of things that could pop up, just like detours, roadblocks, and car troubles can intrude on a road trip. One of the biggest roadblocks to a retirement road trip is taxes. I would call it more of a road closure, in some cases. Remember how long it took to count to a trillion? Multiply that by 33 and you get more than 1 quintillion years. In other words, if we spent a dollar a second trying to pay down our national debt, it would take over 1 quintillion years. The debt clock keeps ticking, but one day soon we will have to do something about it. Either the government will cut spending or raise taxes. Which one do you think is more likely?

Why isn't this information more mainstream? Why aren't we hearing about this every day on the news? Well, it's kind of boring, and nobody wants to hear that their taxes are going to go up. But that doesn't change the fact that it is likely to happen.

If we know that tax rates and brackets are likely to change in the future, all hope is not lost. We can plan ahead for it by taking advantage of strategies that reduce your tax bill and maximize your current tax bracket. I spend a lot of time on tax planning in retirement because taxes have a bigger impact on you when you stop working. A dollar saved in taxes is worth more to you than a dollar earned. Saving as much as you can on taxes also takes pressure off the rest of your portfolio to generate income. The less **risk** you need to take on in order to achieve the growth and income you require, the safer and more durable your portfolio will be.

By planning for future taxes and finding ways to maximize your income while minimizing your tax bill, you are looking ahead instead of behind. If you file your taxes every year by sending your W2s and 1099s to a CPA, you are looking in the rearview mirror of your retirement road trip. By planning ahead for the tax realities that await you in the future, you are looking forward through the windshield of your car. And we all know it is easier to get where you want to go when you are looking ahead. Instead of just looking back at the last year and determining what you can do about it, you can look ahead one, five, 10, or 15 years out, helping you to plan not just how to pay the lowest tax bill *this year*, but how to pay the lowest amount of taxes legally possible over *your lifetime*. That might mean paying more this year or next, but much less in the future.

Your tax situation is a different animal after retirement. Instead of plugging money into a tax-deferred account like a 401(k) that reduces your annual taxable income and grows over time, you are now taking money out of that tax-deferred account and paying full income tax rates on it. Many people think their tax bill will go down in retirement, but often the opposite is true. And down the line when you need to take your required minimum distributions (RMDs), your tax bill could be even *higher*, even if you don't need the money from your RMD for income.

Tax rates are currently at historic lows. The prospect of higher taxes is looming. Many Americans have the majority of their savings and investments in tax-deferred accounts. Put all of those variables together, and the idea of finding a way to reduce future tax bills starts to seem pretty important. Maybe *the most* important thing you can do to prepare for retirement.

But how can you plan to pay fewer taxes in the future? One way is to consider making a **Roth IRA** conversion. Okay, I can see you rolling your eyes and shaking your head and thinking about the big tax bill that would come due. But think about it this way: you will have to pay taxes on your tax-deferred money *anyway*. If you don't do it now, you'll have to do it in the future. And we have already established that the future likely holds higher tax rates and brackets as our national debt crisis continues to grow out of control. So, pay now in a low tax rate environment, or pay later when you don't know what your tax rate or bracket will be?

I'm not saying this is a slam dunk strategy and that everyone should convert today. But I am saying that it is worth considering. There are strategies for approaching a Roth conversion that take advantage of your current tax bracket and leverage your situation to minimize the amount of taxes you pay on your money. The benefits can be tremendous: tax-free income and tax-free growth on converted funds.

If it makes sense, converting your funds to a Roth account can benefit you and your beneficiaries after you pass away. So, does it make sense? Should you convert? My honest answer is, "I don't know." I'm not a conversion cowboy who thinks it is a cure-all for everyone. It depends on your situation, your timeline, your retirement reality, and your goals. When it comes to your money in retirement, nothing happens in a vacuum. Everything affects everything else. Hence the title of this book: *To Roth or Not To Roth?*

This book is focused on examining the financial elements of retirement and using them to help determine if a Roth conversion makes sense. There is no formula or software program or product that will give you a definitive answer. Determining if conversion makes sense for you will require consideration of all the moving parts of your retirement. It is kind of like figuring out the route you are going to take on your road trip. If you have a gas guzzling SUV that can hold a bunch of gear and all the kids, you will need to stick to major roads that have plenty of gas stations along the way. If you are traveling alone and packing light in a Subaru, you might want to venture off the freeway and find areas that are less traveled. It is up to you, and it all depends on your situation.

I know the idea of a Roth conversion can seem alarming or full of uncertainty. This book isn't designed to talk you into a conversion. It is designed to give you information so you can make that determination for yourself. I hope you enjoy reading it and that you find some valuable takeaways to help you on your retirement journey.

Sincerely,
Billy Voyles

Fundamental Wealth Designs

CHAPTER ONE

THE BIG SHIFT

"Nothing happens in a vacuum in life: every action has a series of consequences.
~ Khaled Hosseini

Before we dive into whether a Roth conversion makes sense for you, we need to do some housekeeping. Retiring in today's financial and economic landscape is a different bag than it was for past generations. The whole idea of having to plan for retirement is a new concept for us as individual Americans, and for our nation as a whole. The reason things are so different now is because of everyone's favorite place to invest their money: the 401(k).

Until 1978, the 401(k) didn't even exist. Today, many of those accounts represent the largest investment that people have, aside from maybe your house.

And that's great!—in a way, the 401(k) was a huge success. It helped companies relieve the pressure of having to provide expensive pensions for retired employees, and it allowed people to save and manage (to some extent) their own retirement accounts. On top of that, individual savers could reduce their annual tax bill by saving money in their 401(k) because these accounts are tax-deferred.

Tax deferral is a two-edged sword, however: you don't pay taxes now, but you will pay later when you withdraw the money. With the disappearance of pensions and the rise of defined-contribution plans like the 401(k), the majority of American families are invested in the stock market.[1] As a result, 67 percent of American workers say the nation faces a retirement crisis.[2] The burden of saving for retirement has shifted and that can cause many sleepless nights.

With the responsibility of saving and investing your own money for retirement comes the responsibility of determining when and how you will retire. How much money will you need to save? Will you be able to afford a decades-long retirement? There's no one holding your hand through these decisions; it is up to you to figure it out. Add in a volatile stock market, fluctuating interest rates and bond rates, and inflation, and you can see that preparing for retirement today has become much more complicated than it used to be.

Another key difference between your grandparents' retirement and yours is life expectancy. Just making it to retirement used to be a big deal. Only 56 percent of men made it to age 65 back in the 1950s, and the total number of Americans aged 65 or older was only 12.7 million.[3] You had no real dream for retirement because life during your golden years just didn't last very long.

Compare this to today, where at age 65, a man can realistically expect to live another 17 years and women another 19.8.[4] The number of Americans aged 65 and older is projected to nearly double from 52

---

[1] Saad, Lydia and Jones, Jeffrey M., What Percentage of Americans Own Stock?, Gallup, May 2022 https://news.gallup.com/poll/266807/percentage-americans-owns-stock.aspx Accessed 1/16/2023.
[2] Bond, Tyler et al, Retirement Insecurity 2021, National Institute on Retirement Security, February 2021, https://www.nirsonline.org/reports/retirementinsecurity2021/ Accessed 1/16/2023.
[3] Social Security History, Life Expectancy for Social Security, archival document, https://www.ssa.gov/history/lifeexpect.html Accessed 1/16/2023.
[4] National Center for Health Statistics, Older Person's Health, CDC, August 2021 https://www.cdc.gov/nchs/fastats/older-american-health.htm Accessed 1/16/2023.

million in 2018 to 95 million by 2060.[5] Most people reading this book can expect their retirement to last anywhere from 20 to 30 years.

Before we can answer questions about Roth conversions, how much money you need, and whether you have enough, we need to start at the end of the equation and work backwards. We need to know what you want your retirement to look like, what you expect from your golden years, and what your goals are after you stop working. Once we know what you want, we can start doing the math to figure out how to get it.

Fast Fact: The World Economic Forum reports that most people will live past mandatory retirement age by another 20 to 30 years.[6]

STEP #1: DEVELOP A VISION

Television commercials, brochures, and promotional materials about investment products and retirement tools all have photos of people enjoying retirement. Walking along a beach or having dinner with friends are common scenes. But this is real life, not made-for-TV retirement. So ask yourself, what do you want your retirement to look like?

Do you want to travel less or travel more? Downsize or maintain your current lifestyle? Spend all your money, live on the interest, or preserve a specific amount for a legacy?

Your retirement vision should be based on you, your family, and the things that you like to do, not someone else's definition of what the ideal retirement should look like. Not everyone wants to buzz around the country in an RV.

[5] Profile of Older Americans, Administration for Community Living U.S. Department of Health and Human Services, May 2021 https://acl.gov/sites/default/files/aging%20and%20Disability%20In%20America/2020ProfileofOlderamericans.final_.pdf Accessed 1/20/2023
[6] Nazeri, Haleh, We desperately need to disrupt our approach to retirement saving, World Economic Forum, March 2022, https://www.weforum.org/agenda/2022/03/why-the-concept-of-retirement-needs-to-retire/ Accessed 2/02/2023

- When you close your eyes and picture yourself retired, where are you?
- Who are you with?
- What are you doing?
- How will you spend your mornings?
- Your afternoons?
- What does your ideal evening look like?

Studies find that living a meaningful life with a sense of purpose is fundamental to your well-being during retirement, and strong personal relationships and broader social engagement actually lead to better physical health[7]. After spending a lifetime developing an identity that is focused around career and means of income, retiring without developing a vision can be a shock to the system. It's never too late to identify the kinds of activities that give you a sense of worthwhile fulfillment and the people with whom you want to be spending time.

Fast Fact: Studies consistently show that friendships are as important as family ties in predicting psychological well-being in adulthood and old age.[8]

STEP#2: CREATE A SPENDING PLAN

The first thing people think of when doing retirement planning is the money. They worry, "Do I have enough to retire?" To answer this, don't use

---

[7] Socci, Marco; Santini, Sara; Dury, Sarah; Perek-Bialas, Jolanta; D'Amen Barbara; Principi, Andrea, Physical Activity during the Retirement Transition of Men and Women: A Qualitative Longitudinal Study, NIH National Library of Medicine, August 2021 https://www.ncbi.nlm.nih.gov/pmc/articles/PMC8423544/ Accessed 1/20/2023.

[8] Mayo Clinic Staff, Friendships: Enrich your life and improve your health, Mayo Clinic, January 2022 https://www.mayoclinic.org/healthy-lifestyle/adult-health/in-depth/friendships/art-20044860 Accessed 1/20/2023.

someone else's number. The spending plan must match your retirement vision to support the golden years you've always imagined.

While spending in retirement will look different for everybody, there is a simple way to figure this out for yourself. Developing a spending plan to understand what you're spending now is key to identifying the things that are essential to achieving your retirement vision.

This step includes digging deeper into your expenses by asking yourself which expenses are a *want* and which are a *need*? We will be defining these terms because the first 10 years of retirement are generally when you're going to feel the best, do the most, and possibly spend the most. So, we want to make sure you have what you *need* to be able to do what you *want*. Architects draft blueprints, pilots create flight plans, and writers develop book outlines. Financial advisors design spending plans.

Ideally, you want to track your spending for three to four months. Your spending categories—such as travel, fuel, groceries, clothing—can be broken down into two broader groupings: Needs and Wants.

Needs include the things required by the body for basic survival.
- Food
- Water
- Shelter
- Utilities
- Insurance
- Clothing
- Healthcare
- Medicine/prescriptions
- Transportation

Wants might be essential to the mind and spirit, but they are things the body could live without.

- Travel
- Vacations
- Hobbies
- Charitable donations
- Grandchildren spoiling
- New cars
- Dining out
- RV expenses

To develop a spending plan, look at what you are currently spending every month in the six areas of housing, healthcare, transportation, personal insurance, food, and miscellaneous expenses. Here is a breakdown of these six areas to give you an idea of what kinds of things you should include in each category.

Housing: includes mortgage cost, property taxes, homeowner's insurance, rent, utilities, repairs, maintenance, plus other fees and expenses.

Healthcare: includes medical services, medications, and supplies, plus health insurance.

Transportation: includes vehicle maintenance, fuel, auto insurance, public transportation, and rideshare expenses.

Personal Insurance: includes life insurance, umbrella policies, disability insurance, long-term care, final expenses, or any other insurance.

Food: includes both groceries and dining out.

Miscellaneous: includes outstanding loan payments, credit card payments, entertainment, travel and vacation, hobbies, gifts, education expenses, charitable donations, and any other expenses not listed.

As you start to record all the amounts in these six areas, you might find yourself thinking about how some of these expenses will change once you are retired. You might also realize that an item you thought was a *want* is really a *need*, meaning your retirement won't feel satisfying or meaningful without it. A true plan allows for flexibility and gives a way to finance both *needs* and *wants*.

Fast Fact: One in 3 retirees find their overall expenses were higher than expected.[9]

STEP#3: IDENTIFY THE RETIREMENT INCOME GAP

The **income gap** is the difference between your retirement living expenses and the income from guaranteed sources such as pensions or Social Security. You might also have other sources of guaranteed income such as rental income or payment from an **annuity.**

Living expenses - guaranteed income = the income gap

Breaking down the income into two different types will help inform your decisions for funding the income gap.

To fund your retirement income needs, consider using long-term, guaranteed sources of income that are not in the stock market.[10] Even if a pandemic breaks out during the year that you retire and the market takes a 30 percent nosedive, these income-creating tools can ensure that the expenses you need to survive will still be covered.

---

[9] Retirement Confidence Survey, 2022. EBRI, https://www.ebri.org/retirement/retirement-confidence-survey Page 9. Accessed 4/14/2023.
[10] Guarantees are backed by the financial strength and claims-paying ability of the issuing company.

To fund your retirement income wants a combination of market investments such as stocks, bonds, and mutual funds might be appropriate. During times of market turmoil, as long as your basic expenses are met, you should be able to leave these investments alone as part of your long-term growth strategy. When the market is up or the time is opportune, you may cash in these investments to fund one of your retirement wants.

Fast Fact: During the financial crisis that triggered the Great Recession, the S&P 500 index lost 53% of its value from October 2007 to February 2009, and it wasn't until six years later that the index returned to its pre-recession peak.[11]

Jack and Olive are wondering if they have enough money saved to retire. They know that their bills total $8,070 a month for an annual expense of $96,840. When they sit down and look closer at their needs vs. wants, they get a clearer picture: their basic needs can be met with only $60,000 a year.

"But that doesn't include our trip to Italy," Olive notices.

"No, it does not," says their financial professional. "So that's what we have to identify. How much of the $8,000 a month do you want to have as a sure thing, and how much are you comfortable with as a maybe?"

To answer that question, the financial professional takes them through the retirement income gap exercise. They discover that they will receive a total income of $32,000 from Social Security and another $25,000 annually from Jack's pension. This gave them a total of $57,000 in guaranteed retirement income.

They have no other sources of guaranteed income.

[1] Parker, Kim, and Fry, Richard, More than half of U.S. households have some investment in the stock market, Pew Research Center March 2020 https://www.pewresearch.org/fact-tank/2020/03/25/more-than-half-of-u-s-households-have-some-investment-in-the-stock-market/ Accessed 1/20/2023.

Doing the math, Jack and Olive calculated a retirement income gap of $3,000 a year for their needs and a gap of $36,840 for their wants. This gave them a total gap of $39,840 annually.

"So, how much of this income gap do you want to fund as a sure thing and how much do you want to fund as a maybe?"

"Well, if we're talking about our trip to Italy," says Olive, "I won't feel like I'm living my dream retirement without it. So, I need that trip to be a sure thing."

Traveling to Italy for Olive was not a maybe. She needed to know that it would be a sure thing.

By getting clear about both their retirement vision and their spending, Jack and Olive are now able to choose how to allocate their retirement assets. [12]

STEP #4: WORK WITH A FIDUCIARY

The number one fear of people retiring today is running out of money before they run out of life. Benefit plans that once provided a retirement income for the average American worker have changed. Today, most people won't be receiving a pension, and that shift means there are extra steps for you to take before you can retire with confidence, knowing the money won't run out. You don't have to take these steps alone.

A growing number of financial professionals have dedicated their careers to helping people figure this stuff out. In retirement confidence surveys, when workers in your typical 401(k) savings plans were asked what the most valuable improvements to their plan would be, the most cited answer was better explanations for how much income their savings

---

[12] The above story is a fictional story using actual figures from sources believed to be reliable. This example is shown for illustrative purposes only. Estimated projections do not represent or guarantee the actual results of any transaction, and no representation is made that any transaction will, or is likely to, achieve results similar to those shown.

would produce in retirement[13]. This is the job of a financial professional who specializes in retirement income.

The key thing to realize here is that not all advisors focus on retirement planning. Some of them are better suited to helping you get *to* retirement rather than *through* it. As such, the assets and financial solutions they recommend will reflect that. The **fiduciary** comprises of a duty of care, trust, and loyalty that requires an advisor to serve in the best interest of the client at all times.[14] That means if there are financial products or solutions that will better serve you, a fiduciary must eliminate or disclose all conflicts of interest which might cause the adviser—consciously or unconsciously—to give advice that is not in your best interest. A fiduciary is also required to base their advice *not* on commission fees but on the client's objectives.

This is why fiduciaries begin *not* with the numbers but with a series of questions designed *to get to know you.* Generally speaking, fiduciaries are more concerned with getting to know the person and establishing a relationship of trust rather than selling you a certain product or investment. First, they will take the time to get to know you so that they can understand the worries and concerns particular to you. If retirement income is one of those worries, then they'll be able to recommend a financial tool that can get you a regular, recurring income stream if that's what you need. They will also take the time to alert you to all the risks you could face given today's elongated retirement time. These risks involve other kinds of losses besides those you could experience in the stock market, risks such as increasing taxes, inflation, and long-term care. He or she can also help you file for Social Security in a way that compliments your overall plan.

---

[13] EBRI, 2022 Retirement Confidence Survey, https://www.ebri.org/retirement/retirement-confidence-survey Accessed 1/20/2023.
[14] Peirce, Hester M., Outsourcing Fiduciary Duty to the Commission: Statement on Proposed Outsourcing by Investment Advisers, Securities and Exchange Commission, October 2022, https://www.sec.gov/news/statement/peirce-service-providers-oversight-102622 Accessed 1/20/2023.

If your advisor is not able to help you coordinate all of these things, then it's likely that they do not specialize in helping someone get all the way *through* retirement.

Because retirement planning has gotten more complicated than it used to be, more is being asked of you. In return, you might also expect more from your advisor. Are they talking to you about market risk, Social Security, and how to get an income stream? Can they give you a written plan where it tells you in black and white when you can retire? Can they serve as your fiduciary?

By taking the time to consider all the factors that can impact your happiness in retirement, including both financial and non-financial matters, your nest egg will stand a better chance of supporting the kind of retirement that you've envisioned.

Fast Fact: Your choice of a financial advisor can dramatically affect your retirement savings due to variations in fees, compensation, and conflicts of interest. [15]

TO ROTH OR NOT TO ROTH: Figuring out what you want to do with your retirement is the first step in figuring out whether a Roth conversion makes sense for you. With the advent of the 401(k), many Americans have most of their retirement savings in the stock market. The need for a stable, guaranteed, tax-efficient income is at odds with the inherent volatility and risk of the stock market. By defining your goals in retirement and determining what you want to do, and working with a fiduciary professional you can trust, you can start to create a well-coordinated plan that helps you achieve your goals.

---

[15] The Pew Charitable Trusts, Issue Brief: Choice of Financial Adviser Can Dramatically Affect Retirement Savings, July 2022 https://www.pewtrusts.org/en/research-and-analysis/issue-briefs/2022/07/choice-of-financial-adviser-can-dramatically-affect-retirement-savings Accessed 1/17/2023.

HOW DO YOU WANT TO RETIRE?

- Figure out what you want your retirement to look like.
- Develop a spending plan.
- Identify your income gap.
- Work with a fiduciary who specializes in retirement income creation.

CHAPTER TWO

INCOME

"The question isn't at what age I want to retire, it's at what income."
~ George Foreman

Imagine your retirement savings as a reservoir of water. You have spent years and years adding buckets of water to the reservoir. You have built a dam to keep it all in, and you have sealed up as many of the leaks as possible.

Now, after storing and holding all that water, how do you access it when it comes time for you to use it? Do you take it out, bucketful by bucketful, like you put it in? Carrying water is hard work! You want to spend your time enjoying the fruits of your labor, not doing more work.

Figuring out what to do with your retirement savings is a lot like figuring out how to access that water. It's great that you have a big account balance in your 401(k) or IRA, but those accounts are like the water in the reservoir. How do you access them? What is the best and most efficient way to get the water to your house, where you will actually use it?

This is one of the concepts that confounds so many retirees. Your 401(k) or IRA is not a retirement plan. It is not an income plan. It is an account—and many, if not all, of the dollars in that account may be invested in the stock market. Your goal in retirement isn't to keep adding water to the reservoir. Your goal in retirement *is to create an income stream* that provides you with enough money to meet your goals without depleting your reservoir.

There are all kinds of pop-finance marketing phrases that oversimplify how to position yourself for retirement. You may have heard of a 60/40 balance, the four-percent rule, or target date funds. Those strategies or the concepts behind them may or may not work for you, but that's not the point. You *need* to know that you can spend your money to meet your needs and that your money will last as long as you do. Some retirees fear running out so much, they're afraid to spend their own money. So, we created the idea of a *spending plan* where we can determine how much you can afford to spend every month. The spending plan frees up time and energy, and it lowers stress levels and budgeting headaches.

Think about it: you have spent your entire life earning, saving, and investing your money. You have been doing the *opposite* of spending it. You have been accumulating it, growing it, and saving it. When you retire, those are the years you have been saving it for. You have been saving for your retirement lifestyle, and now you have to learn how to spend your money instead of accumulating your money. It is a huge paradigm shift, and one that is difficult for many people to make.

You may have heard advice such as "live off the interest while preserving **principal**." But is it safe to stay in the market during today's times? The advent of the 401(k) resulted in millions of dollars being poured into market investments. Now, that money is coming out as the boomer generation retires. This makes the market more volatile than ever before. Combine that with our changing interest-rate environment and the complexity of today's longer retirement, and you're tasked with a difficult responsibility: deciding how much pressure to put on your investment portfolio.

While every adviser has their own secret sauce when it comes to designing an income plan, some of the best solutions didn't exist 50 years ago. This chapter is designed to show you more options than what you may have been exposed to. You don't have to keep your money in the market, watching it go up and down, taking on more risk than you are comfortable with or aware of. Having a customized and solid retirement plan means giving yourself permission to spend your money in retirement so you can enjoy your golden years and not have to worry about running out of money.

The beauty of being able to guarantee your income in retirement means that you can be more aggressive or growth-oriented with the money that you haven't set aside for income. You can hit the brakes on risk for your income money and hit the gas on the other stuff. And it all starts with knowing which financial phase you are in and making adjustments along the way.

Fast Fact: Only 4 in 10 workers surveyed by the Employee Benefit Research Institute said they had thought about how much to withdraw from their savings and investments for retirement.[16]

WHAT FINANCIAL PHASE ARE YOU IN?

Have you ever wondered why financial advice about saving for retirement varies so much from one advisor to another? This can make it difficult to know who to trust or what to believe.

---

[16] 2022 RCS Fact Sheet #3 Preparing For Retirement In America, EBRI, 2022. https://www.ebri.org/docs/default-source/rcs/2022-rcs/rcs_22-fs-3_prep.pdf?sfvrsn=e5c83b2f_4 Accessed 2/21/2023

One straightforward way you can wade through the riff-raff is to identify what financial phase you're in and then choose your investment strategy accordingly.

Broadly speaking, every investor who saves for retirement finds themselves going through two financial phases in their life. Those two phases are the **accumulation phase** and the **distribution phase**. What follows is the when, how, and who of the investment strategies you'll use during these phases and the kinds of professionals who can help guide you.

ACCUMULATION PHASE

WHEN: During your working years, you've been accumulating and growing your assets. In the business of financial planning, we call this your *accumulation phase*. If you're disciplined, or if you've had the foresight to set up automatic withdrawals, then you've probably gotten pretty good at accumulation.

HOW: This financial phase benefits from long-term **passive investment strategies such as buy-and-hold and dollar-cost averaging.** Basically, you keep putting away the money, and over time the money grows. Whether the stock market goes up, down, or sideways, as long as you don't touch this money, your account should move upward, which is exactly the outcome you want.

WHO: For this phase, it's common to work with a fund manager provided by the HR department of your employer, especially if you have a 401(k) or retirement plan with an employer match. You might also work with a stockbroker or a broker-dealer for help with the buying and selling of investments. You may even try doing this kind of investing by yourself using online financial services. You are, after all, responsible for making the lion's share of the contributions.

Fast Fact: According to a report by FINRA, investor knowledge in the United States is low.[17]

DISTRIBUTION PHASE

WHEN: During retirement, investors enter the *distribution phase.* This phase begins when you're no longer putting money into your portfolio or retirement accounts; instead, *you're taking the money out.* This fundamental shift changes everything you thought you knew about a sound investment strategy.

HOW: During this phase, investors are advised to make their allocation selections based on *preservation first* and *growth second.* Some advisors even usher their clients through a third phase, known as **the preservation phase,** five to 10 years prior to when their clients need this money for income. During the preservation phase, the portion of money required for your income *needs* is reallocated into financial instruments that better protect this money from market volatility.

However, given today's longer retirement and the likelihood of a long-term care event, most people can't afford to get out of the market altogether. They require some combination of short-term and long-term investing strategies and income planning tools that employ low to moderate risk.

WHO: To be successful during the distribution phase requires much more finesse and forethought than the strategies used during the accumulation phase. Market risk isn't the only threat to your retirement portfolio: it can also be damaged by tax inefficiencies, long-term care catastrophes, and the problem of required distributions from tax-qualified

[17] Lin, Judy T, et al, Investors in the United States: The Changing Landscape, FINRA, December 2022, page 2. Choice of Financial Adviser Can Dramatically Affect Retirement Savings, July 2022. https://finrafoundation.org/sites/finrafoundation/files/NFCS-Investor-Report-Changing-Landscape.pdf Accessed 3/31/2023.

retirement accounts. For this reason, you'll want to work with an advisor who specializes in this phase.

Distribution specialists are trained to ensure that your money lasts for the rest of your lifetime. They do this by coordinating your investment decisions with your distribution strategy for greater efficiency and more robust portfolio durability. They know how to look out for unintended side-effects such as increased taxes and how to give you advice about claiming your Social Security. Ideally, these advisors are also independent and able to give you access to a full spectrum of investments that include both securities and insurance tools.

- Insurance-only agents can get you access to income vehicles but not market investments.
- Broker-dealers can give you access to market investments, but typically not insurance tools.
- Independent investment advisors who also have their insurance license—and most of them do—can give you access to a full spectrum of investments, including market securities, insurance tools, and active investment strategies.
- An investment advisor representative is held to the fiduciary standard and legally required to give you advice that is in your best interest.

You might also want to inquire about the advisor's firm and the scope of its services. Can they give you access to a tax specialist? An estate planning attorney? Can they create active strategies and execute tactical asset management? Are they able to run a Social Security optimization report to help you get a filing strategy?

In short, can your advisor get you the access you need to investments, strategies, and solutions specific to the financial phase you're in?

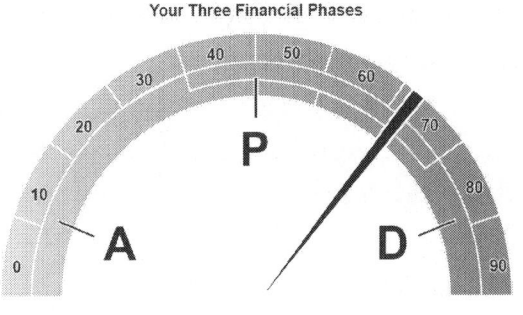

Source: Magellan Financial

3 WAYS TO GENERATE INCOME FROM YOUR INVESTMENTS

Because this financial phase is all about how to take the money out of the accounts, it's not just important to choose the right investments; it's also about timing. What the market happens to do during the years just before and after you retire can have a significant impact on how much you'll have left to fund your retirement income. For this reason, you may want to use a combination of strategies.

What follows is the When, How, and Who of strategies for filling the income gap.

OPTION #1 USING A PASSIVE INVESTMENT STRATEGY

WHEN: A **passive investment strategy** broadly refers to a buy-and-hold strategy with minimal trading in the stock market. Index investing is another common form of passive investing, where investors strive to replicate the returns of a broad market index such as the S&P or Dow Jones indices. The use of mutual funds is also common. This strategy is most effective during your accumulation years when the investor has a time horizon of 10 years or more.

HOW: In order to be successful, this strategy requires a long time horizon and a strong stomach committed to riding the market ups and downs. *While this strategy has the potential to earn the most, it also has the potential to lose the most.* The amount that you put into the investment is not guaranteed to be there when you need to take it out. This could make passive strategies problematic if you want a reliable income.

There are withdrawal strategies designed to mitigate the risk, most notably the **4 percent rule.** This rule was designed to answer the question, *how much can you safely withdraw from your portfolio every year without going broke?* **While 4 percent annually was once thought to be safe, experts now find that it may be unsustainable, as it assumes (among other things) that a retiree keeps more than 50 percent of their portfolio in stocks.**[18] The reason for this has to do with today's rising interest-rate environment, high market volatility, and high inflation rate.

WHO: Passive investment strategies may not be ideal for the person at or approaching retirement. While lowering the withdrawal rate to a more modest percentage is one solution, that doesn't satisfy the income needs of most people. You also shouldn't be willing to accept 50/50 odds when heading into retirement. Thankfully, better options exist.

Fast Fact: The 4% rule for income withdrawal has now shriveled to only 2.4% for investors taking a moderate amount of risk in today's post-pandemic world. [19]

---

[18] Iacurci, Greg, Retiring soon? Why the popular 4% withdrawal rule may be a bad idea, CNBC, April 2021, https://www.cnbc.com/2021/04/13/why-the-popular-4percent-withdrawal-rule-may-be-a-bad-idea-for-retirees.html Accessed 8/28/2023.
[19] Rusoff, Jane Wollman, "Wade Pfau: Pandemic Tears Up 4% Rule," Think Advisor, April 2020, https://www.thinkadvisor.com/2020/04/14/wade-pfau-virus-crisis-has-slashed-4-rule-nearly-in-half/ Accessed 2/22/2023

Dan and Connie had always been good savers. They had invested throughout their careers and for the last decade had stayed in the stock market. Their portfolio had reached a value of $750,000 and they were very proud of the work they had done to get it there.

Their retirement savings was the most money they had ever accumulated, and using the 4-percent rule to fill their income gap seemed like a reasonable way to fund their retirement. It would only be a withdrawal of $30,000 from their $750,000 account, they reasoned, and with the market going up, they felt they would have no problem with cash flow. They set up automatic withdrawals with their broker so the same amount would come out of their account each year, and it would even be adjusted annually for inflation.

That would have all been great if things went as planned. But, as is often the case, life threw them a curveball. In the year they retired, the market fell by 20 percent. Their portfolio value hit $600,000 before they had withdrawn any money. After their $30,000 came out, their portfolio was valued at $570,000. Four percent of that would give them $22,800. The automatic withdrawal of $30,000 was closer to 5.5 percent of their portfolio value. .

Between February 19 and March 23, 2020, the market fell by 34 percent.[20] Dan and Connie quickly realized their withdrawal strategy wasn't suited to the realities of the market. Today, they need a better plan. [21]

OPTION #2 USING INCOME VEHICLES

WHEN: While the market gives us an opportunity to generate increasing returns, it can also put you at risk of receiving a decreasing

---

[20] Statista Research Department, Change in performance of S&P 500 during COVID-19 pandemic vs previous major crashes. Statista, January 2022. https://www.statista.com/statistics/1175227/s-and-p-500-major-crashes-change/ Accessed 2/22/2023.

[21] The above story is a fictional story using actual figures from sources believed to be reliable. This example is shown for illustrative purposes only. Estimated projections do not represent or guarantee the actual results of any transaction, and no representation is made that any transaction will, or is likely to, achieve results similar to those shown.

income during market declines. One solution designed specifically for investors approaching retirement who have a shorter timeline is income annuities.

HOW: An income annuity is a flexible insurance tool that uses an indexing method to give you market-linked gains without direct exposure to market risk. It has low to no fees, the money grows tax-deferred, and it passes to your beneficiaries without **probate. The indexing method allows you to address inflation and receive a *potentially* increasing income while also receiving principal protection**. The value of the account is guaranteed never to go down due to market loss, but the potential for market-linked returns is still there.

WHO: Income annuities can be very flexible. They can be used with or without an income rider to generate a steady or increasing income for someone in retirement. They can also be used as a savings vehicle for someone near retirement who wants to protect a portion of their funds. Certain types of income annuities have accumulation periods during which the interest accumulates tax-deferred.

When I meet with people who are ready to plan their retirement, I ask them if they want to *hope* or *know* that their income will last them the rest of their lives. I think you can already guess what the answer is. People want to *know* that they will have enough money to live the life they are accustomed to. They want to *know* that if an expensive healthcare bill comes their way, or if the stock market loses double digit percentages, that they will be alright. They don't want to guess. They want to know. And one of the best ways to know what your income will be is by using an income annuity. There is no other alternative out there that I am aware of—whether it be an investment, a bank instrument, bonds, whatever—that is literally a contract between you and a company that will pay you for the rest of your life. Of course, you can *hope* if you want to, but hope isn't a strategy.

Because so many different types of annuities exist, be sure to talk to your advisor about the advantages and disadvantages. Typically speaking, these are long-term insurance tools with limited access to **liquidity. Guarantees are based on the claims-paying ability of the issuing company,** so shop around and compare different insurance companies to get the benefits and features you best suited to your needs.

Fast Fact: Research shows that fixed-rate deferred annuities average an interest rate over four times that of bank CDs.[22]

OPTION #3 USING AN ACTIVE INVESTMENT STRATEGY

WHEN: Investors with a shorter timeline may want to limit their exposure to market loss. While a passive strategy operates under the assumption that you must stay in the market because you can't miss the best days, an active investment strategy operates under the directive to limit the worse days.

The investor with a shorter timeline doesn't have time to recover from market loss. The mathematical reality of **account value restoration** shows us why: we can never get back to even by receiving a gain equal to the loss.

For example, we often think that to recover from a 50 percent loss, we need a 50 percent return. In reality, we need an even greater return to recover from any loss, regardless of how big or small. Take a look at the following visual to understand why.

[22] Annuities, Kiplinger, 2022. https://www.kiplinger.com/retirement/annuities Accessed 2/23/2023.

Source: Magellan Financial. Not indicative of investment performance.

Once your account loses, the compounding muscle of your portfolio becomes crippled. You're no longer starting with the same base amount, and so it takes more investment energy to restore your account to its previous vigor. It also takes more time. It took over a decade for the average investor practicing buy-and-hold to get back to even after 2008 [23]

HOW: An active strategy seeks to limit loss by ongoing buying and selling based on market conditions and economic indicators. Instead of receiving 100 percent of both gains and losses, the goal of an active

[23] Roberts, Lance, After A Decade, Investors Are Finally Back to Even, Seeking Alpha, Feb. 2020. https://seekingalpha.com/article/4324760-after-decade-investors-are-finally-back-to-even Accessed 2/23/2023.

strategy is to limit loss in exchange for a limited portion of the gains. For example, an active strategy might seek to capture 70 percent of market gains and no more than 40 percent of market losses.

WHO: An **active management** strategy gives specified objectives tailored to the investor at or nearing retirement. Your money is managed, meaning your holdings are actively adjusted. If the market is heading south, your money manager has the ability to move your holding to cash. This gives you help during times of volatility and the potential for improved risk-adjusted returns. This strategy comes with a management fee in exchange for a shorter timeline and the peace of mind you get knowing someone is actually managing your money.

BEWARE: Many investors operate under the assumption that because they have a fund manager or pay fees to their broker, their money is being professionally managed. Unfortunately, this is not the case with your typical mutual fund manager. Specific language in the fund prospectus requires a fund to invest at least 80 percent of its assets in the type of investments implied by the fund name, a rule known as SEC rule 35d-1.[24] **This means that even if your broker or fund manager knows that the market is tanking, they can't do anything to help you.**

Fast Fact: Research suggests that if you plan to travel and lead an active lifestyle, then you'll need to ratchet up your overall retirement budget by 6%.[25]

Pearl and Frank were ready to retire. They both liked their jobs but had been looking forward to leaving them at the same time so they could spend

[24] U.S. Securities and Exchange Commission, Frequently Asked Questions about Rule 35d-1 (Investment Company Names) https://www.sec.gov/divisions/investment/guidance/rule35d-1faq.htm Accessed 2/23/2023.
[25] Bond, Tyler, Doonan, Dan, and Kenneally, Kelly, Retirement Insecurity 2021, The National Institute on Retirement Security, Feb 2021, https://www.nirsonline.org/wp-content/uploads/2021/02/FINAL-Retirement-Insecurity-2021-.pdf Accessed 2/23/2023

the rest of their lives relaxing, traveling, and enjoying each other's company. On their 45th wedding anniversary, they retired together and had a big party.

The next morning, they took a look at their budget. They knew how much they would be getting from Social Security, and Pearl even had a small pension from her federal employer. They did some math and figured they needed about $2,000 a month more than their guaranteed sources of income were providing. That didn't seem like too big of a deal. They had some savings and investments, and it didn't seem like a big stretch to siphon money off of those accounts to supplement their needs. It was only $2,000 a month, they reasoned.

Toward the end of the year, just before the holidays, the market took a hit, and Pearl and Frank's savings, which were heavily invested in the stock market, went down by over 20 percent. In addition, they had withdrawn over $20,000 to fill their income gap over the year. The small sum of $2,000 a month added up quickly over the course of a year. They were also withdrawing while the market was going down, which compounded their loss and made it much harder, if not impossible, for them to recover. They suddenly felt in over their heads and began to fear that their retirement would not look like what they had hoped. [26]

If you have an income gap when you retire, as many people do, then it is imperative that you have a plan to fill it. What may seem like a small amount, as illustrated in the story above, can add up quickly and diminish the ability of your savings to provide you with income. If you are heavily invested in the market, a year or more of market losses can devastate your portfolio while you are still relying on it for income. This is why *hoping* you have enough money isn't a good plan. Pearl and Frank could have easily

[26] The above story is a fictional story. The results obtained are hypothetical and do not represent the investment of actual funds nor the performance of an actual account. Past performance is never indicative of future investment results. The performance presented does not reflect the application of all fees or trading costs.

set up a guaranteed source of income or an active management strategy with some of their savings so the behavior of the market wouldn't dictate the quality of their lifestyle.

Retirement is a time you should enjoy. Everyone's idea of enjoyment is different, but whatever it means to you, you should be able to achieve it after working and saving your entire life. Part of enjoying your time means not having to worry about money. Why watch the markets and wonder whether you'll have enough money each year to make it to the next when you could set up a plan that delivers you the income you need no matter what?

TO ROTH OR NOT TO ROTH: Understanding the financial phase you are in can help you find the right balance of risk and safety you need in your portfolio. By determining your income gap, and then creating a strategy to reliably fill that gap, you can create the financially stable situation you need to determine whether a Roth conversion is the right option for you. An active strategy can be tailored to fund your income wants. By matching non-risk investments to your income needs, and risk investments with a longer timeline to your income wants, you'll stand to gain a greater probability of success during today's uncertain times.

CALCULATE YOUR INCOME GAP
- Put your income needs and wants into a quantifiable format.
- Identify all known sources of guaranteed income.
- Calculate your income gap.

CHAPTER THREE

TAXES IN RETIREMENT

"Being smart doesn't mean you have all the answers, but it means you are willing to find them."
~ Anonymous

If you know anything about Roth accounts, then you know they have a lot to do with taxes. Specifically, the principal and the growth in a Roth account can be withdrawn tax-free after a certain amount of time has passed, and/or after you reach the age of 59½. But not everyone has been saving in a Roth account from the get-go.

Many Americans have the bulk of their retirement savings in tax-deferred accounts like 401(k)s and **traditional IRAs**, and it is easy to understand why. You get a kind of two-for-one benefit by reducing your annual tax bill while also saving for retirement. And all the while your money is growing, and you don't have to pay taxes on it—for now.

The growing number in your tax-deferred account isn't real, however. The dollars in it are real, numbers don't lie. But when you go to *spend* that money, all those years of tax-deferral catch up to you. A dollar isn't a dollar when you take it out of a tax-deferred account. A good chunk of that dollar belongs to the IRS, and the size of the chunk is whatever size they tell you it is.

Assuming a 24 percent tax rate and a $1 million account, you don't really have $1 million to spend. In reality, you only have $760,000 or $680,000 or even $650,000 depending on your tax bracket because a certain percentage of every dollar belongs to Uncle Sam. And if history repeats itself and tax rates go up, you might have even less.

We know that tax laws and rates change over time. We know what the tax rates are now, but we don't know where they will be in the future. All signs point to the probability of rising taxes. The more you can reduce your tax liability now, the less income your portfolio has to generate in the future to support your lifestyle—meaning you can assume less risk with the same outcome.

Thinking about what you can *earn* isn't enough. The real test is understanding how to think like a tax planner by looking at your portfolio in terms of **how much money you get to *keep*.**

Fast Fact: Income taxes can be your single largest expense in retirement.[27]

TAX ME NOW, TAX ME LATER, TAX ME SOME, TAX ME NEVER

There are four types of money when it comes to your retirement savings. For the purposes of this chapter, we are also including Social Security in the equation because it is a tax-advantaged source of income. By learning how to keep below certain income thresholds, you can learn how to diversify your retirement income from a tax standpoint to maximize your tax-advantaged income and keep more of your money.

---

[27] FINRA, Taxation of Retirement Income, 2023, https://www.finra.org/investors/learn-to-invest/types-investments/retirement/managing-retirement-income/taxation-retirement-income Accessed 1/31/2023

Taxable: You will pay taxes every year on the money inside taxable accounts.

This income is reported as dividend or interest income on your 1099 tax form. Most people have at least some money in taxable accounts. Examples of these accounts include your savings, money market savings account, bank CDs, individual bonds, individual stocks, and brokerage accounts that are *not* retirement accounts.

The drawback of taxable accounts is that you must pay taxes on any interest earned even if you don't plan to spend the money. For example, if your bank CD earned 2 percent for the year, but you're in a five-year contract, you would still owe taxes on the amount of interest earned before the CD matures. This can eat into your profits, making it difficult to keep up with inflation, particularly with bank products. If you have too much money in taxable accounts, then you might want to work with a knowledgeable tax professional who can help you do tax *planning* rather than simply tax *paying*.

Fast Fact: As of September 2022, Americans held $6.3 trillion in untaxed wealth inside their 401(k) and $11 trillion inside their IRAs.[28]

Tax-deferred: You won't have to pay taxes on the money in these accounts until you take it out, or when you reach a certain age and the IRS requires you to withdraw a certain amount.

Tax-deferred accounts are sometimes called qualified accounts. Why? Because they qualify for a certain kind of tax treatment. This deal allows you to save the money *before* the income has been taxed, allowing it to grow tax-deferred until you go to spend it *later*. If you're participating in

[28] Investment Company Institute, 401(k) Resource Center. ICI Global. September 2022. https://www.ici.org/401k Accessed 5/18/2023.

your company's retirement plan such as 401(k) or Thrift Savings Plan, 403(b), 457, IRA, SEP IRA, Simple IRA, Spousal IRA, or profit-sharing plans, then congratulations, you will qualify for retirement taxes.

These taxes come due when you take this money out. If you don't need the money right away and you keep growing it, you will have to spend it eventually according to the rules. The tax-deferred retirement accounts listed above all have required minimum distributions—known as the RMD—that become due once you reach a certain age. The age of this RMD has changed twice with the passing of the SECURE Act, first to age 72, and now as of January 2023, to age 73.[29] Because of the SECURE Act 2.0, the RMD will eventually become age 75 by the year 2033.[30] This is the age at which you must take this money out, but there's no law that says you can't take it out earlier.

Why would you want to take the money out earlier? Because if this account grows too large, future withdrawals (or even just your RMD obligations) could cause a lot of problems later such as a higher tax rate, a bigger tax bill, a smaller amount of Social Security income, and a hike to your Medicare premiums.

Thankfully, you do have the option of moving this money into a different account where the money can be withdrawn tax-free.

Fast Fact: Between the ages of 59½ and 73, there is no rule that restricts how much or how little you must take out of your tax-deferred retirement account.[31]

---

[29] Senate Finance Committee, SECURE 2.0 Act of 2022 Title I, Jan 2023, https://www.finance.senate.gov/imo/media/doc/Secure%202.0_Section%20by%20Section%20Summary%2012-19-22%20FINAL.pdf Accessed 1/4/2023.
[30] Ibid.
[31] IRS, When Can a Retirement Plan Distribute Benefits? April 2023, https://www.irs.gov/retirement-plans/plan-participant-employee/when-can-a-retirement-plan-distribute-benefits Accessed 6/21/2023.

Tax-advantaged and tax-free: Tax-advantaged accounts give you tax-preferential treatment on your retirement income while tax-free accounts give you tax-free income.

Everybody gets some form of tax-advantaged income during retirement thanks to Social Security. At least 15 percent of this income will be paid to you tax-free, and some people receive all of this income tax-free. How much of your Social Security income will be taxed depends on your *provisional income*, which we will define below.

All Roth IRA accounts will give you tax-free retirement income. This is because the money is taxed when it's going in, so it won't be taxed again when it's coming out. **Every dollar you take out of a Roth will cost you zero dollars in taxes.** With a Roth, even the gains earned by the money comes to you tax-free, which is why many people consider doing a Roth conversion.

A Roth conversion is when you move the money *out* of a traditional IRA or retirement account and *into* a Roth account. While you first must pay the tax debt owed, and there are rules, every dollar you convert from a traditional IRA into a Roth IRA can come back to you in the form of tax-free retirement income later, and that includes any gains earned.

Here is the cliff-notes version to make this easier to remember:
Taxable accounts = tax me now.
Tax-deferred accounts = tax me later.
Tax-advantaged = tax me some.
Tax-free accounts = tax me never.

Fast Fact: About 40% of people who get Social Security have to pay income taxes on their benefits.[32]

HOW YOUR SOCIAL SECURITY BENEFIT IS TAXED

Learning how to optimize your Social Security benefit plays a big role in gaining a tax-efficient withdrawal strategy. Because the income thresholds for this benefit haven't changed since 1980, most people will be taxed on this benefit. But there are ways to mitigate the bite, and with proper planning, it might even be possible to receive more of this income tax-free.

As little as 15 percent and as much as 100 percent of your Social Security income can be received tax-free. Up to 85 percent of your benefit may be taxed, and it will be taxed at your highest marginal income tax rate. This came as a big surprise to Pete and Ingrid.

Pete and Ingrid retired with a provisional income of $90,000 a year. Their income included Jack's pension of $40,000 a year, Ingrid's RMD of $30,000 a year, and one-half of their combined Social Security benefits at $20,000.

Pete and Ingrid's provisional income exceeded the $44,000 threshold, so 85 percent of their Social Security benefits were taxed at their highest marginal tax rate. Because they were in the 22 percent tax bracket, and 85 percent of their Social Security benefit was $34,000, they were paying $7,480 a year in taxes on their Social Security income.

However, there is an unintended side effect of this. Pete and Ingrid were receiving $7,480 less in income each year! To make up for this, and so they

[32] SSA "Social Security Administration: Retirement Benefits" 2023 https://www.ssa.gov/pubs/EN-05-10035.pdf Page 11 Accessed 4/20/2023.

could meet their expenses, Ingrid withdrew more money from the IRA. At a 22 percent tax rate, she took out $9,589 to compensate for the taxation.

Had that $9,589 been allowed to stay in the IRA, it would have continued to grow tax-deferred. Every year as the **cost-of-living adjustment (COLA)** goes up, they get an increased tax bill, requiring more and more money to come out of the IRA. Over time, this could easily amount to anywhere from $300,000 to $1 million in lost assets due to Social Security taxation[33].

Pete and Ingrid need a better plan.

The two things to know when determining how your Social Security benefit will be taxed are your *provisional income* and your *income threshold*. Let's take a look at each of these key areas.

PROVISIONAL INCOME FORMULA

Provisional income is also referred to as **combined income** by the IRS or **SSA**. The magic formula for figuring this out is the total of three things:

1. Your adjusted gross income. This includes income from your job, rental income, royalties, interest, dividend payments, business income, alimony payments, pensions, and annuities. This does NOT include your Social Security income.
2. Your non-taxable interest income. This includes any sources of tax-free interest income such as tax-exempt bond funds and municipal bonds.
3. Half of your Social Security income. This is where you add your Social Security income, but only HALF of this income is counted. The formula looks like this:

[33] The above story is a fictional story using actual figures from sources believed to be reliable. This example is shown for illustrative purposes only. Estimated projections do not represent or guarantee the actual results of any transaction, and no representation is made that any transaction will, or is likely to, achieve results similar to those shown.

Your adjusted gross income + any non-taxable interest income
+ ½ of your Social Security income
=
Your provisional income

INCOME THRESHOLD:

The Social Security Administration bases the amount of your taxation on *income thresholds* dependent on your filing status. These are set by law and not adjusted annually.

The following income thresholds are current as of 2023[34]. **If you file a federal tax return as an "individual"** and your *provisional income* is:

- less than $25,000, then you may pay zero taxes on your Social Security benefit.
- between $25,000 and $34,000, then you may have to pay income tax on up to 50 percent of your benefits.
- more than $34,000, then you may have to pay income tax on up to 85 percent of your benefits.

- **If you file a joint return,** and you and your spouse have a provisional income that is:
    - less than $32,000, then you may pay zero taxes on your Social Security benefit.
    - between $32,000 and $44,000, then you may have to pay income tax on up to 50 percent of your benefits.
    - more than $44,000, then you may have to pay income tax on up to 85 percent of your benefits.

[34] SSA. "Retirement Benefits." https://www.ssa.gov/benefits/retirement/planner/taxes.html. Accessed 1/11/2023.

- **If you are married and file a separate tax return,** then you probably will pay taxes on your benefits.

Another complication is the addition of taxes at the state level. There are a handful of states that tax your Social Security income, however, some of them make special provisions. For example, Missouri, West Virginia, and Vermont only tax benefits if your income exceeds certain (generous) thresholds, and Utah allows a tax credit for a portion of the benefits, beginning in 2021.

Your advisor should keep track of the changing rules for your state. For example, in 2022, the 12 states that taxed Social Security income were, in alphabetical order: Colorado, Connecticut, Kansas, Minnesota, Missouri, Montana, Nebraska, New Mexico, Rhode Island, Utah, and Vermont.[35]

Fast Fact: Studies find that a more tax-efficient withdrawal strategy can help boost your nest egg anywhere from 1 to 11%.[36]

GET A WITHDRAWAL STRATEGY

Once you're retired and living off your benefits and the money in your various accounts, you have a choice:

1. Withdraw this money willy-nilly with a tax-inefficient strategy.
2. Follow conventional wisdom and put off spending those tax-deferred dollars for as long as possible.
3. Work with an advisor who specializes in retirement distribution strategies to get a customized withdrawal strategy.

[35] Mengle, Rocky, and Block, Sandy, 12 States That Tax Social Security Benefits, Kiplinger, November 2022. https://www.kiplinger.com/retirement/social-security/603803/states-that-tax-social-security-benefits Accessed 1/11/2023.

[36] Geisler, Greg, Harden, Bill, Hulse, David S., A Comparison of the Tax Efficiency of Decumulation Strategies, Financial Planning Association (FPA), March 2021. https://www.financialplanningassociation.org/article/journal/MAR21-comparison-tax-efficiency-decumulation-strategies Accessed 1/11/2023.

Obviously, no one wants to run out of money before running out of life. Yet most people choose option two because they want to put off the odious task of paying taxes for as long as possible. Really, who can blame you?

And yet, the Journal of Financial Planning finds that for most retirees, **a more tax-efficient withdrawal strategy can help boost your nest egg anywhere from 1 to 11 percent when compared to conventional wisdom or non-customized strategies.**[37] For some people, this might include waiting to file for Social Security, allowing this tax-advantaged source of income to grow as big as possible, while spending those tax-deferred accounts now while taxes are effectively on sale. For other people, it might include Roth conversions to take full advantage of your low tax-brackets during the early years of retirement.

The optimal approach must be tailored to your situation, but the rewards can increase how long your wealth will last in retirement.

How much longer?

That same study in the Journal of Financial Planning found that tax-efficient withdrawal strategies **can add years of life to your portfolio without assuming additional risk.**[38]

A tax-efficient withdrawal strategy isn't rocket science, but it definitely takes some mathematic gymnastics. The best path forward may not be the one you think.

If you were to begin withdrawing money from your retirement accounts today to provide you with income, which one would you dip into first? Everyone's situation is different, and there are always exceptions to the rule, but I have found that the following withdrawal order makes sense for many of the people who I meet with.

---

[37] Geisler, Greg; Harden, Bill; Hulse, David S., A Comparison of the Tax Efficiency of Decumulation Strategies, Financial Planning Association (FPA), March 2021, https://www.financialplanningassociation.org/article/journal/MAR21-comparison-tax-efficiency-decumulation-strategies Accessed 5/4/2023.
[38] Ibid.

- Start with your **qualified money.** This is usually the account(s) with the largest balance in it, since people may have been saving, investing, and getting employer matches in them for decades. This money is tax-deferred, which means you haven't paid taxes on the principal or the growth. Every dollar that comes out of these accounts is subject to income tax. Since we are currently in a historically low income tax environment, using this money sooner rather than later may be beneficial, and can also help reduce the amount you are forced to withdrawal in the form of RMDs down the road. Once your RMDs kick in, you lose a significant amount of control over how and when you pay taxes on this money. Additionally, if you find yourself in a low tax bracket because one spouse has retired earlier, or because your RMDs haven't started yet, etc., then withdrawing money for income from your qualified account(s) can be more affordable than having to pay higher taxes on this income later if you find yourself in a higher tax bracket.
- After your qualified money, it might be tempting to use tax-free money. Lower or no taxes is good, right? Yes, it's good, but it may not be the best step to take, yet. Often, transitioning to **non-qualified money** for retirement income can help maintain a lower tax environment for you. How is this possible? Remember, you have already funded non-qualified accounts with after-tax money. You only owe capital gains taxes on non-qualified money, which is often lower than regular income tax.
- The last money to touch for income is your **Roth or tax-free money.** By using your qualified and non-qualified money to prevent lazy tax brackets, optimize your income, and take advantage of historically low income tax rates, you can allow your tax-free money to grow. It is also easier and more beneficial to transfer Roth money to your beneficiaries after you pass away.

Fast Fact: Studies find that 40% of wealthy households—defined as having a combined income from Social Security and savings averaging $7,242 a month—are at risk of not being able to maintain their lifestyle due to taxation.[39]

TO ROTH OR NOT TO ROTH: Following conventional wisdom, you may be tempted to withdraw money from your non-qualified or Roth accounts first, and your tax-deferred money last. In practice, however, that kind of withdrawal order can get you into hot water, increasing your risk of running out of money before you run out of life. Instead of risking your future income, you can work with an experienced professional with expertise in customizing tax-efficient withdrawal strategies. Remember, just as important as how much you have is how much money you keep.

GET A TAX-EFFICIENT WITHDRAWAL STRATEGY

- Identify how much of your future retirement income is in tax-deferred accounts.
- Get a tax-efficient claiming strategy for your Social Security.
- Investigate how spending tax-deferred accounts earlier rather than later could reduce your exposure to higher taxes in the future.

[39] Chen, Anqi, and Munnell, Alicia H., How Much Taxes Will Retirees Owe On Their Retirement Income? Center for Retirement Research at Boston College, November 2020, Page 15, https://crr.bc.edu/wp-content/uploads/2020/11/wp_2020-16.pdf Accessed 5/04/2023.

CHAPTER FOUR

ROTH IRA CONVERSIONS: SEED OR HARVEST

"The best time to plant a tree was 20 years ago. The second best time is today."
~ Chinese Proverb

To Roth or not to Roth, that is the question. The idea of reducing your future tax bill to insulate yourself from the uncertainty of rising market volatility, variable interest rates, and longer lifespans is an attractive one. Turning the ticking tax timebomb in your traditional IRA or 401(k) into a tax-free source of safety and security could set you and your beneficiaries up for a much smoother financial future.

Roth conversions are a hot topic these days because, as we explored in Chapter One, the economic and financial landscape of America has changed since your parents and grandparents retired. More people are invested more heavily in the stock market, there has been a huge shift away from pensions to defined-contribution accounts like 401(k)s, and the burden of securing an income in retirement has fallen more squarely on the shoulders of the individual. In a best-case scenario, a Roth conversion can help remove the risk that taxes pose on your retirement cashflow, and help you easily pass your financial legacy on to your beneficiaries.

It isn't as easy as "yes" or "no," however. Whether or not a Roth conversion makes sense for you depends on several different factors. If it were easy, everyone would be doing it and there would be no drawbacks. But a Roth conversion comes with a price: income taxes.

The way I like to explore this decision-making process with people is by asking, "If you were a farmer, would you rather pay taxes on the seeds you buy to plant in the spring? Or on the harvest that you gather at the end of the season?"

The obvious answer is you would want to pay taxes on the seed. It would be cheaper, and whatever profit you made on the harvest would be tax-free. A Roth conversion can work in a similar way in that when you move money into a Roth account, you must pay income taxes on it. This is like paying taxes on the seed. But down the road, when you withdraw the money, you don't have to pay taxes on any of the gains the account makes, or on the principal you put in (since you already paid taxes on it when you converted). This analogy simplifies the process, but it gives you an idea of how a Roth conversion might be beneficial to you.

We saw in the previous chapter about tax efficiency and withdrawal order that spending your tax-deferred dollars last may not be the best approach for your income needs in retirement. This chapter will show you how to leverage today's tax laws to help you protect your investments from being overtaxed.

While it was Benjamin Franklin who said nothing is certain except death and taxes, you might extend this to say, *"increasing taxes."* This could also be true of your IRA because of required minimum distribution (RMD) withdrawal rules.

Even if you don't want to spend this money, even if you have plans to leave your IRA to your spouse or family or a charity, the rules for IRA distributions say you MUST spend this money. As you age, the IRS *increases* the amount you must withdrawal because getting older means you have less time to spend it. So as your account gets bigger and you grow older, you'll be required to spend more of this money even if you don't want to.

This will theoretically mean an increasing tax bill because your income will increase. This can also trigger a higher marginal tax rate, a reduction in the amount of Social Security income you get to keep, and an increase to your Medicare Parts B and D.

There is good news, however. This is one area of your retirement plan where *you may have more control than you think.*

Fast Fact: Only two-thirds of American workers surveyed in 2023 are confident they will have enough money to live comfortably in retirement.[40]

THE WINDOW OF TAX OPPORTUNITY

Let's not confuse *paying* your taxes with *planning* for your taxes. Paying your taxes is what you do every year by the deadline of April 15. By then, it's usually too late to do anything but pay what you owe.

Planning for your taxes means looking ahead—sometimes as long as 10 years into the future—and using current tax law to your advantage.

So, looking ahead, how many people think that tax rates will be going *down* during the next 15 years?

Nobody.

How many people think taxes will be going *up*?

---

[40] Retirement Confidence Survey, 2023, EBRI and Greenwald Research, https://www.ebri.org/docs/default-source/rcs/2023-rcs/2023-rcs-short-report.pdf Accessed 11/21/2023.

Everybody.

When you think about retirement spanning 20 to 30 years, and you look at where we are today as compared to where we've been, it becomes pretty obvious which direction we're headed. The question is, how high will they go?

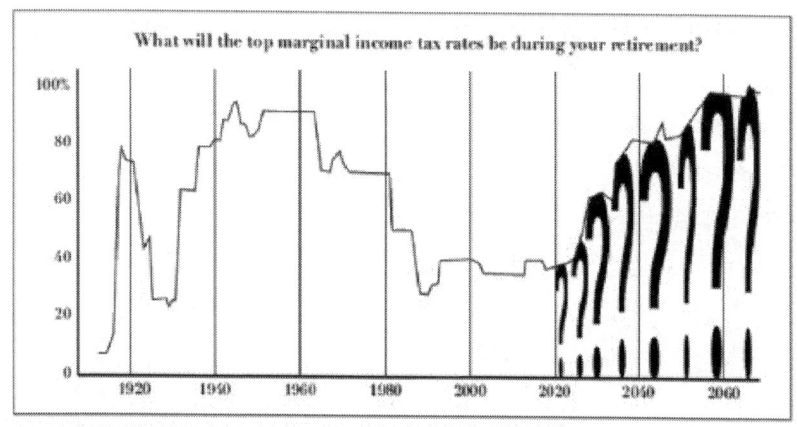

What will the top marginal income tax rates be during your retirement?

Source: Magellan Financial using data from the Urban-Brookings Tax Policy Center, "Historical Individual Income Tax Parameters: 1913 to 2018."

On November 16, 2017, the House of Representatives passed the Tax Cuts and Jobs Act to reform the individual income tax codes. This act lowered tax rates on wages, investment, and business income, and it changed the standard deductions for millions of filers, nearly doubling the standard amount. But these individual income-tax changes are set to expire on December 31, 2025, when tax brackets will revert to 2017 levels.[41] This will be a significant day for most taxpayers.

Twenty-three provisions are set to expire, so most taxpayers will see a tax hike unless provisions are extended.[42]

[41] El-Sibaie, Amir, A Look Ahead at Expiring Tax Provisions, Tax Foundation, January 2018 https://taxfoundation.org/look-ahead-expiring-tax-provisions Accessed 6/23/2023.
[42] Ibid.

What this means for you is that right now we have a window of opportunity where it's possible to do some real planning. Taxes are at historically low levels. They aren't going to stay this low forever.

The window of opportunity is squeezed even further by the fact that most people only have between the ages of 59½ and 73 to do something about the tax-deferred money in their 401(k)s and traditional IRAs. Before the age of 59½, you can't access your money without incurring penalties. And at age 73, your RMDs kick in and you *must* withdraw an ever-increasing amount of money each year, which is subject to income taxes, or you're faced with penalties. Within that window, however, you have the most control over how to organize and position your money for tax efficiency.

Let's start by taking a look at how RMDs might affect you.

Fast Fact: The highest marginal tax rate for 2023 was at a historic low. The highest rate ever seen was 94% in 1944-1945. It remained in the 50% to 90% range until it went down in 1987 to 38.50%.[43]

THE WHO, WHEN, AND WHAT OF THE RMD

Retirement accounts have rules about when and how much money you may put in. Some of these accounts also have rules about when and how much you must take out. The required minimum distribution (RMD) is the amount of money you are required to withdraw once you hit a certain age. What follows is the who, when, what, and why of the RMD.

WHO: Anyone who owns a retirement account such as a 401(k) or an IRA account that is not preceded by the words "Roth" may be required

---

[43] Tax Policy Center, Historical Highest Marginal Income Tax Rates, May 2023, https://www.taxpolicycenter.org/statistics/historical-highest-marginal-income-tax-rates Accessed 6/23/2023.

to take an RMD. This includes traditional IRAs and IRA-based plans such as SEPs, SARSEPs, and SIMPLE IRAs. It does not apply to Roth or non-qualified accounts. It may also not apply if you are still contributing to your 401(k).

WHEN: When you reach a certain age, your RMD comes due. The age of this RMD has changed twice since the passing of the SECURE Act, first from age 70 ½ to age 72, and now as of January 2023, to age 73.[44] Because of the SECURE Act 2.0, the RMD will eventually become age 75 by the year 2033.[45] It's wise to expect they will continue to change every few years as people continue to live longer.

WHAT: To calculate the exact amount of your RMD, the IRS uses a division formula based on two things: 1) your account's balance at the end of the preceding year, and 2) the number of years that you're expected to live. Your RMD amount is then calculated by dividing your tax-deferred retirement account balance as of December 31 of last year by your life expectancy factor.

For example, if your account balance at the end of the year was $500,000 and you're expected to live another 27.4 years, then your RMD would be $18,248 for that year.

The IRS calculates your life expectancy by looking at the Uniform Lifetime Table. This table calculates the number of years that you have left to pay the taxes you owe on this amount of money. Because we're living longer, the IRS updated the tables with new rates going into effect beginning 2022. The longer you live, the shorter amount of time you have to pay the taxes owed, so the withdrawal rates (RMD%) *increase* as you age.

---

[44] Senate Finance Committee. SECURE 2.0 Act of 2022 Title I, Jan 2023, https://www.finance.senate.gov/imo/media/doc/Secure%202.0_Section%20by%20Section%20Summary%2012-19-22%20FINAL.pdf Accessed 1/4/2023.
[45] Ibid.

FOR USE BY IRA OWNERS IN 2022 AND BEYOND

\multicolumn{3}{c}{Uniform Lifetime Table}
Age	Life Expectancy Factor	RMD% Equivalent
72	27.4	3.65%
73	26.5	3.77%
74	25.5	3.92%
75	24.6	4.07%
76	23.7	4.22%
77	22.9	4.37%
78	22	4.55%
79	21.1	4.74%
80	20.2	4.95%
81	19.4	5.15%
82	18.5	5.41%
83	17.7	5.65%
84	16.8	5.95%
85	16	6.25%
86	15.2	6.58%
87	14.4	6.94%
88	13.7	7.30%
89	12.9	7.75%
90	12.2	8.20%
91	11.5	8.70%
92	10.8	9.26%
93	10.1	9.90%
94	9.5	10.53%
95	8.9	11.24%
96	8.4	11.90%

\multicolumn{3}{c}{Uniform Lifetime Table}
Age	Life Expectancy Factor	RMD% Equivalent
97	7.8	12.82%
98	7.3	13.70%
99	6.8	14.71%
100	6.4	15.63%
101	6	16.67%
102	5.6	17.86%
103	5.2	19.23%
104	4.9	20.41%
105	4.6	21.74%
106	4.3	23.26%
107	4.1	24.39%
108	3.9	25.64%
109	3.7	27.03%
110	3.5	28.57%
111	3.4	29.41%
112	3.3	30.30%
113	3.1	32.26%
114	3	33.33%
115	2.9	34.48%
116	2.8	35.71%
117	2.7	37.04%
118	2.5	40.00%
119	2.3	43.48%
120	2	50.00%

Source: 2022 IRS Uniform Lifetime Table

WHY: Because retirement accounts are tax-deferred accounts, you deferred the taxes—meaning you didn't pay them yet. The RMD is the amount of money you must withdraw and then pay income taxes on. But perhaps the more important question to ask yourself is, "Why are we talking about this now?" We are devoting a chapter to this subject because when you do take this money out, it gets taxed as ordinary income. And that could trigger a series of ugly tax consequences.

Taking an IRA distribution, no matter how big or small, will increase your annual income. This has the potential to set off the following:
- An increase to your marginal tax rate.
- An increase in the amount of overall income taxes you pay.
- An increase in the amount of your Social Security benefit that is taxable.

- An increase to your Medicare Parts B and D premiums.

How much will your taxes go up? Crossing over the threshold into a new marginal tax rate can increase your overall tax bill by as much as 83 percent under current law, or 67 percent using 2017 tax brackets.

Married Filing Jointly			
Old Law		**Tax Cuts and Jobs Act**	
10%	$0-$19,050	10%	$0-$19,050
15%	$19,050-$77,400	12%	$19,050-$77,400
25%	$77,400-$156,150	22%	$77,400-$165,000
28%	$156,150-$237,950	24%	$165,000-$315,000
33%	$237,950-$424,950	32%	$315,000-$400,000
35%	$424,950-$480,050	35%	$400,000-$600,000

67% Increase (Old Law 15%→25%) / 83% Increase (TCJA 12%→22%)

Source: Urban-Brookings Tax Policy Center. Recent History of the Tax Code, "How did the Tax Cuts and Jobs Act change personal taxes?"

What's the deal with Medicare Parts B and D? Once you become eligible for Medicare, you will pay a premium each month, automatically deducted from your Social Security. Most people pay the standard premium amount; however, if your modified adjusted gross income goes above a certain threshold—even if this is due to a one-time withdrawal—then you trigger an increase to your payment known as **IRMAA** (Income Related Monthly Adjustment Amount). This adjustment also means an increase in Medicare Part D.

One common trigger of IRMAA is the RMD, so make sure your advisor is aware of how much retirement income you are required to pull out.

Can you take out your RMD early? Yes. You can take out this money early before you turn age 73 and any time after you reach age 59½. You can also take MORE money out of your IRA than required by the RMD, but you can't take less. Failing to take out the full amount, or failing to withdraw the RMD by the deadline, will cost you a penalty tax of 25 percent.

At age 62, Terry had half of a million dollars in his IRA when he retired. He worked for the federal government, so he had a pension and an amount from Social Security to rely on after he stopped working. With those two sources of guaranteed income in place, Terry planned to leave his IRA money to his wife and family after he passed away. He retired and continued to let the account accumulate, leaving it in the stock market. Over the next 10 years, it grew to just over $1 million.

Terry was over the moon about doubling his IRA. But he soon found out there was more to the story. After those 10 years, Terry turned 72 years old. Now, he was required to start taking his RMD. He withdrew the required $39,000, which was reported to the IRS as income. That extra income pushed him into a higher income-tax bracket, increasing his taxes; at the same time, he also owed more money in Social Security taxes—at the new higher rate.

Terry quickly began to understand that he was trapped in a tax nightmare. If he doubles his money again at the age of 82, his RMD could require that he withdraw 5.44 percent of this money based on the current life expectancy table. That income would move him up again into an even higher tax bracket, causing even more of his Social Security to be taxed, more of his pension to be taxed, and more of his IRA money to go to Uncle Sam.

This is not at all what Terry had in mind when he saved this money.[46]

---

[46] The above story is a fictional story using actual figures from sources believed to be reliable. This example is shown for illustrative purposes only. Estimated projections do not represent or guarantee the actual results of any transaction, and no representation is made that any transaction will, or is likely to, achieve results similar to those shown.

HOW TO GET RID OF YOUR RMD

The rule of 72 tells us how long it will take for your money to double given a fixed rate of interest. For example, if your account is making 6 percent with a balance of $1 million and you retire at age 61, then you're going to see that account double in 12 years. That means when you reach age 73, your RMD is going to be based on a $2 million account.

Now, take a look at the Uniform Life Expectancy table and notice how the number of years (the distribution period) keeps getting lower while the percentage of your account balance (the amount you're required to withdraw) keeps getting bigger. Mathematically speaking, if you're dividing a number that keeps getting bigger by a number that keeps getting lower, **the amount of your RMD will keep getting higher.** As you get older and need this money less, you'll be required to take out more money from an account that you'd potentially intended to leave for someone else, meanwhile triggering those ugly tax consequences.

There is a way to get rid of your RMD. If you do some thoughtful planning and take care of these pesky taxes ahead of time, you can fund an account that would allow you and your beneficiaries to withdraw contributions tax-free at any time. And once you've funded this strategy for at least five years, even the interest can be accessed without having to pay a penny in taxes.

Fast Fact: Once your RMD becomes due, for every dollar you fail to withdraw the IRS will charge a 25% penalty. [47]

---

[47] IRS, Retirement Plan and IRA Required Minimum Distributions FAQs, March 2023, https://www.irs.gov/retirement-plans/retirement-plan-and-ira-required-minimum-distributions-faqs#:~:text=the%20required%20deadline%3F-,(updated%20March%2014%2C%202023);timely%20corrected%20within%20two%20years Access 5/5/2023.

Using the marginal income tax rates as a guide and working with an advisor, it's possible to pull out a strategic amount from your IRA every year while staying below your income threshold to fund a Roth. Even if your income is higher than the maximum the IRS allows for regular Roth contributions, there is an IRS-sanctioned method for funding a Roth during retirement. Withdrawals from your IRA will be taxed as income at your current rate because a Roth is funded with post-tax money. But because Roth withdrawals are not taxed later, even on the interest they accumulate, it can be a better deal for someone in a rising-tax environment.

Roth conversions are not for everyone. They require proper tax planning and an advisor who takes a holistic approach because conversions could trigger unintended tax consequences if they are not carefully analyzed. In some cases, consulting with multiple professionals might be appropriate. This chapter is designed to help give you an education about Roth conversion benefits. When you convert to a Roth, you receive significant tax advantages:
- No RMDs.
- Tax-deferred growth.
- Tax-free interest.
- Tax-free income.
- Tax-free money to your beneficiaries.

All the money you put into a Roth can be taken out again without being reported on your 1040 tax form. Furthermore, when your account earns interest, you will not receive a 1099 form requiring you to report those gains, and even if your account doubles, you will have no RMD! All interest earned, whether it is from dividends or capital gains, are distributed tax-free as long as the account has been opened for at least five years. This is sometimes known as the "five-year rule" for the Roth IRA.

This can be a lot of information to digest, but the good news is that no one is expecting you to make this decision alone. An independent fiduciary financial professional can help guide you through the decision-making process to see whether a conversion makes sense for you. The following indicators can also help you feel out if a conversion might be right for your portfolio.

ROTH CONVERSION INDICATORS & PLANNING IDEAS

- Folks with variable income streams, such as business owners, may benefit from a Roth conversion. If your income ebbs and flows from year to year, you can take advantage of lower-income years by doing a partial conversion while in a lower tax bracket.
- Someone who has just started a new business venture and is transitioning into receiving income from that business may want to consider converting. During the early years, for example, you may be showing very little income on your tax form. This could also put you in a lower-than-normal tax bracket, which could be a beneficial time to convert some funds.
- Anyone who has reason to believe they may be subject to higher marginal tax rates in the future should weigh the option. If you know your income will be increasing to the point that it puts you in a higher tax bracket, taking advantage of the lower tax bracket you are in now to convert some funds could make sense.
- Often, the maximum tax-efficiency of a Roth conversion comes before your RMDs begin. Once your funds are converted to a Roth, you are not required to pay RMDs on them during your lifetime.
- It may also make sense to convert before age 63 to avoid costly impacts to your Medicare IRMAA charges for Parts B and D. These premiums are based on your income. Medicare has a two-year look-back provision, so converting before age 63 can help avoid that scenario.
- If you have had the unfortunate experience of losing a spouse this year, you may want to consider a Roth conversion while you can still

file a married-joint tax return. The conversion income can be on the final joint tax return, allowing you to take advantage of the lower rates and higher income limits of a married-joint tax return.

There are plenty of myths and stray pieces of information floating around the internet, and around the water cooler, about Roth conversions and Roth accounts. Instead of relying on what you hear secondhand, you should meet with someone who is experienced and educated about Roth conversions. For example, the SECURE 2.0 Act now allows employees to put employer-matched retirement savings into a Roth account. Contributing to a Roth account is not the same as *converting* your existing tax-deferred money into a Roth.

Because there is so much to be aware of when considering a Roth conversion, it is important you don't try to do it by yourself. It may seem simple enough to just transfer money from one account to another, but by now you should realize that the implications of that transfer can be wide reaching and affect your tax bill, your income, and your overall net worth. The ultimate goal of a Roth conversion is to give you more flexibility in retirement while minimizing your tax bill. But in order to achieve this goal, you need a clear plan that makes sure you stay within the parameters of a successful conversion.

Perhaps the most important thing to consider is that the money you withdraw from a non-Roth account, even if it is intended for a conversion, will be taxed as regular income. That essentially means the balance in your traditional IRA or 401(k) isn't really all yours. A good chunk of it belongs to Uncle Sam.

In most cases, I advise people to try and pay the taxes from a source other than the converted funds account so that they don't eat too drastically into their retirement savings. It is also important to avoid the tax consequences of being pushed into a higher tax bracket while you are converting. That taxable income is reported on your 1040, and if you enter a higher tax bracket, your marginal tax rate goes up, as well. By working with someone experienced in Roth conversions, you can determine the most efficient way to convert your funds—or you might decide that a conversion doesn't make sense for you, after all.

Fast Fact: A Roth IRA conversion involves moving assets from other non-Roth retirement accounts into a Roth IRA.[48]

It is important to remember that a Roth conversion is not an *all or nothing* endeavor. In fact, in order to stay in the lowest tax bracket possible while you convert, it often makes sense to execute a series of smaller, annual conversions over a defined period of time to spread out the income tax. While you may want to move as much money as you can into your tax-free bucket of funds, you need to be smart about it. If you end up paying too much in taxes, it might not make sense to do the conversion at all.

Joe had worked for nearly 30 years as an anesthesiologist. His career had been long and lucrative, and when he was getting ready to retire, his 401(k) had just over $1 million in it. Joe felt great about that. At his family Christmas party that year, his brother-in-law, who was a CPA, suggested that Joe think about converting his retirement savings to a Roth IRA.

"You won't have any income taxes in the future when you take the money out. You could have a tax-free retirement," he said.

Joe liked the sound of that.

---

[48] IRA Roth Conversion. Vanguard. https://investor.vanguard.com/investor-resources-education/iras/ira-roth-conversion Accessed 10/3/2023.

That spring, when he retired, Joe had a big party and invited all his friends and family to celebrate. He was so excited and confident in his financial future that he decided making it tax-free would be the cherry on top of the sundae. The day after his party he moved all his money to a Roth IRA.

He had a wonderful summer traveling with his wife and visiting as many national parks as they could. They bought an RV so they could camp in style. Later that year, at the next family Christmas party, Joe told his brother-in-law that he had taken his advice.

"I converted to a Roth, and I haven't worried once about withdrawing money. Thanks for the advice!"

"How much did you convert?" Joe's brother-in-law asked.

"All of it!"

His brother-in-law nearly spit out his drink.

"Joe, I didn't mean you should convert the whole thing at once. Your tax bill in April is going to be enormous."

Joe called his CPA the next day to ask him if it was true. Unfortunately, it was, and there was nothing he could do about it now. He would have to withdraw a huge chunk of his converted funds and pay a much higher marginal tax rate than he normally did.[49]

Converting his funds to a Roth account may have been a good move for Joe, but instead of doing it all at once, spreading the conversion amounts over five or more years may have been a better plan for him. By converting $200,000 each year over five years, Joe likely would have been in a much lower tax bracket and would have been able to keep a lot more of his money in his pocket. As it was, Joe lost a good chunk of his principal to taxes *and* the potential growth that amount could have achieved.

[49] The above story is fictional and for illustrative purposes only. Your own experience may vary.

PASSING IT ON

A Roth conversion can be useful to you during your lifetime, but did you know it can also be one of the best ways to pass on a financial legacy to your beneficiaries? The SECURE 2.0 Act allows for the beneficiaries of Roth accounts to inherit the money tax-free, and they don't need to withdraw the money for up to 10 years. That means it can grow tax-free for up to a decade.

This is one of the primary reasons that many people structure their retirement income withdrawal order so that they use their tax-free Roth money last. The more they can leave in that account and the longer they can let it grow, the more tax-free legacy they can pass on after they die.

A Roth conversion can be a complex undertaking. The potential costs and tax implications, recent changes to tax laws, and cost/benefit analyses are a lot to keep track of on your own. In a rising tax environment, the benefits of a Roth conversion may very well outweigh the costs. It isn't the right choice for everyone, but it might be the right choice for you. The best way to find out is to talk to an experienced financial planner before you make any permanent decisions.

In a best-case scenario, a Roth IRA can be a real gift to both yourself and your beneficiaries because when you go to spend this money, nothing happens! You don't owe income tax on the interest or on the money you take out, so the amount of your annual income as reported to the IRS and Social Security does not change. Your Social Security is not taxed at a higher rate, your marginal tax rate doesn't go up, and there is no change to the cost of your Medicare benefits.

Fast Fact: For savers over the age of 50, you can now contribute an additional $7,500 to a 401(k), 403(b), or other qualified retirement plan on top of the $22,500 federal limit.[50]

TO ROTH OR NOT TO ROTH: A Roth conversion is all about paying taxes while you are in the lowest-possible income tax bracket to maximize the principal and growth potential of your money. It is like the question posed earlier: Would you rather pay taxes on the seed or the harvest? It is important to be strategic and determine whether the known tax rate you are paying now is likely to be lower than the one in the future. Do you think taxes are going to go up?

DIVERSIFY YOUR TAX LANDSCAPE.

- Forecast your RMD to figure out whether the income will be usable or excess.
- Open up a Roth IRA and begin funding it to get the five-year clock ticking.
- Diversify your tax landscape so that you have optimum sources of tax-free and tax-advantaged retirement income.

[50] IRS, Retirement Topics - 401(k) and Profit-Sharing Contribution Limits, Nov 2023 https://www.irs.gov/retirement-plans/plan-participant-employee/retirement-topics-401k-and-profit-sharing-plan-contribution-limits Accessed 5/06/2023.

CHAPTER FIVE

SECTION 7702 - LIFE INSURANCE
Life Insurance for the living

"Before anything else, preparation is the key to success."
~ Alexander Graham Bell

Life insurance, in my opinion, could benefit from being called something else. The options available today are so much more broad reaching, comprehensive, and customizable than the options of the past that many of these policies and products didn't even exist a short time ago. There are huge opportunities for retirees to benefit from life insurance products *while they are still living.*

Along with all those options comes the burden of choice, however. Reviewing everything that is available can get complicated. The same product can have different costs or benefits, it can begin coverage at different times depending on the person who is being insured, and the same ratings can mean different things depending on the carrier. You also have different rider options and benefits exclusions to be aware of, and three different types of approval depending on your health.

To help you understand these choices, financial professionals in the industry have dedicated their careers to learning the ins and outs of insurance tools. It's a challenge because life insurance constantly changes as new options are being added yearly. This is good news for the consumer because as more people retire, more products are being designed to help solve some of the financial problems common to people at this stage of life.

- Concerned about income for a surviving spouse?
- Looking for an accumulation tool outside of the stock market?
- Apprehensive about rising taxes?
- Worried about long-term care?
- Wanting to leave a legacy?

Yes, life insurance can help you solve all those problems. Its benefits extend far into retirement and beyond. This chapter is here to help you increase your knowledge about an asset class that often goes underutilized.

Fast Fact: It's difficult for consumers to find objective financial information because the industry spends over 400 times more on marketing dollars than federal agencies spend on financial education.[51]

TRADITIONAL LIFE INSURANCE: TERM VS WHOLE

If you understand the pros and cons of home ownership versus renting, then you've already got a basic understanding of our first life insurance subject: term versus whole. Let's start with the facts and then go into the advantages and disadvantages of each.

---

[51] Consumer Financial Protection Bureau, Financial Literacy Report, March 2022, page 2, https://files.consumerfinance.gov/f/documents/cfpb_financial-literacy-fy-2021_annual-report_2022-03.pdf Accessed 1/17/2023.

Term Coverage

The purpose of a term policy is to cover the big bills in the event of life passing too quickly. This type of insurance pays a tax-free death benefit to your beneficiaries should you die during the term of your policy.

For example, if you're the breadwinner for your family with a $1 million term policy, and you die unexpectedly in an automobile accident, a term policy would pay out the $1 million death benefit to your spouse. Your family would continue living in their house, meeting the financial obligation of the household, without the added stress of financial pressures on top of their grief. Imagine what a huge gift that would be to your family.

Term policies are known for being affordable and are ideal for people ages 20 to 45. For as little as $10 a month, you can purchase a policy that would pay out a $1 million death benefit to your family. There may also be situations where someone in their early 50s might need to take out a policy with a hefty death benefit, but the cost of these policies only increases the older you get because the insurance company assesses the risk of you dying and charges accordingly. For the older working person, other options should be considered.

A term is the length of time that you are covered. The most common term is 30 years, but 10 and 20-year term policies are also available. Term policies cost the same amount every month (or year) and these policies stay in force as long as you keep making the payments. There is also no point in paying *more* than the required amount because you aren't building equity in the policy. You are simply paying a set amount of money in exchange for the peace of mind you get knowing that should the unexpected happen, your family will be okay.

What happens once the term is *over* depends on the type of term policy you have. In some cases, you can still receive benefits! That's why it's important to work with an agent who will explain and offer a full menu of options.

For example, some types of term policies offer a return of premium (ROP) option where, if you outlive the policy term, then the money you paid will be refunded. While you'll pay considerably more for an ROP policy, you can look at it as a way to save money now that you'll receive later in life, while at the same time protecting your family.

Another option is to continue the policy once the term is over. There are two ways you can do this.

1. At the end of the term, the policy converts to an ART policy—which stands for annual renewable term insurance. The good news is you'll receive coverage without having to reapply or take another medical exam. The bad news is the cost you'll be paying can go up dramatically because people become more expensive to insure as they age.
2. At the end of the term, instead of converting to an ART, the policy converts to a permanent policy. You'll still receive continued coverage without the medical exam, but with a permanent policy, the price never changes for the rest of your life. This can be a valuable asset to have later in life as medical issues tend to start cropping up and you become more difficult to insure.

Advantages:
A low, regular cost for a large death benefit.
Affordable insurance for someone just starting their career.
Tax-free money for your family.
No probate.
No investment or management fees.
May receive a return of all premiums paid.
May have the ability to continue the policy.

Disadvantages:
Coverage is temporary, based on the length of the contract.
No build-up of cash value to use later in life.

> **Fast Fact:** Among parents who have life insurance, 68% of them feel financially secure; only 47% of parents without life insurance feel secure.[52]

Whole Life

The purpose of a whole life policy is to cover a person's insurance needs for their *whole* life. It doesn't expire until you do. This is a financial solution that gives you two things: a death benefit for your family and a cash value benefit for you.

You already understand how a death benefit works—the money is paid out to your beneficiaries in the event of your passing. With a whole-life policy, this death benefit will cost you more. For instance, if you have a budget of $100 a month, term coverage would pay out a death benefit of $500,000. Whole life coverage would only give you a $150,000 death benefit for that same $100. The reason for this has to do with the equity you are building up in your policy.

In the world of life insurance, the *cash value* of a policy is the monetary benefit you can access while you are still alive. This money is best accessed as a loan so you can receive it income tax free. Accessing this money now *does* reduce the death benefit, but you always have the option of paying this money back. When you do, your account is *credited* with an amount of interest, allowing that account to grow back with more vigor. Once the loan is paid up, it no longer reduces the death benefit amount.

Because this gets a little tricky, sometimes people get confused about how much their policy is worth. A whole-life policy has two values: the *cash account value* and the *death benefit value*. You don't get both amounts. Upon your passing, your beneficiaries will receive the higher of the two values. For example, if you have a $100,000 death benefit and a $50,000 cash value, your family will receive $100,000.

If having access to tax-free funds is important to you in retirement, while you are alive, and before you die, then you should ask your insurance agent about today's newer insurance options.

Life insurance has been around for over 200 years, and whole life products are very old. Back in 1979, the Federal Trade Commission (FTC) did a three-year study on whole life after people complained about their fee disclosures and rates. It was found that while the companies were paying out dividends every year, the rates of return offered were several percentage points *below* alternatives readily available in the marketplace.[53] It was because of this report that a newer type of life insurance policy was created, which is exactly what we will cover next.

Advantages:

Insured for the life of the policyholder.
Premiums remain steady.
Builds up equity in a cash-value account.
Ability to spend this money tax-free.
Death benefits for your family or beneficiary.

Disadvantages:

[53] Federal Trade Commission Library, Testimony of Michael Pertschuk, Chairman, FTC, pages 3 – 5, July 1979, https://www.ftc.gov/legal-library/browse/life-insurance-cost-disclosure Accessed 3/01/2023.

Whole life policies cost more than term.
Potentially lower death benefit.
Newer, more efficient options for cash-value accounts exist.

Fast Fact: 40% of wealthy households—defined as having a combined income from Social Security and savings of at least $3,000 a month—are at risk of not being able to maintain their lifestyle due to taxation."[54]

THE UNIVERSE OF UNIVERSAL LIFE

As an adult moves through their working years, they hopefully become more successful, gaining more assets and more responsibilities. They also might find themselves climbing into a higher tax bracket. This makes it imperative to investigate your options for tax-advantaged savings vehicles.

Universal life policies were designed to help solve the problems of someone advancing in their career. They can offer you a way to insure and protect your family in the event of an early death, while also offering a way to accumulate funds tax-deferred outside of the stock market. Unlike a traditional IRA or Roth IRA, they don't have income limits or contribution limits. They also don't demand that once you reach a certain age, you take out a certain amount of money.

Like whole life, these policies last a lifetime, so they typically cost more to fund than a term policy, but in return, they give you more—even more than whole life.

There are four kinds of universal life policies:

UL – Universal Life

---

[54] Chen, Anqi, and Munnell, Alicia H. *How Much Taxes Will Retirees Owe On Their Retirement Income?* Center for Retirement Research at Boston College. November 2020, page 15. https://crr.bc.edu/wp-content/uploads/2020/11/wp_2020-16.pdf Accessed 7/08/2021.

GUL – Guaranteed Universal Life
VUL – Variable Universal Life
IUL – Indexed Universal Life

The differences between these four types have to do with how they are structured. In general, we can put them in one of two categories:

1. The UL and GUL are designed specifically to generate the biggest *death benefit*.
2. The VUL and IUL are designed to generate the biggest cash *value*.

Your choice of policy should be based on the goal you are trying to achieve.

Universal Life and Guaranteed Universal Life

The goal of a UL and GUL policy is to build up the largest possible death benefit over the life of the policy. These policies are very flexible—you can add additional money to fund them whenever you want to, and the funds will go toward plumping up the death benefit. You might even think of them as term policies on steroids.

Universal life (UL) is a lower cost option for people who want to buy the most amount of coverage for the least amount of dollars. It offers a low, fixed rate of interest that, generally speaking, has a floor of 0 to 2 percent, so it will never go lower than that.

The guaranteed universal life (GUL) offers a guaranteed death benefit so that regardless of how the interest credits accumulate, you're still guaranteed to have a certain death benefit amount. However, in the world of life insurance, guarantees are expensive, so keep in mind that this version does cost more.[55]

[55] Guarantees are backed by the financial strength and claims-paying ability of the issuing company.

Before you purchase a UL or GUL policy, please be aware of the advantages and disadvantages:

Advantages:
Insured for the life of the policyholder.
Fixed-rate of interest.
Guaranteed interest options are available.
Larger death benefit for your family.
Can pay additional premiums to increase the death benefits.
Interest accumulates tax deferred.
Benefits are paid to your family tax-free.
Affordable insurance for the person of advanced age.

Disadvantages:
No cash value build-up options.
Little to no indexing options.
Must be healthy to qualify.

Indexed Universal Life and Variable Universal Life

The goal of an IUL and VUL policy is the opposite of the previous two policies. Instead of paying a *lower* amount of money for a larger death benefit we're designing a policy with a *smaller* death benefit to achieve a *greater* cash accumulation value for your situation.

There are two ways to do this.
1. The IUL uses an indexing method for accumulation with principal protection features.
2. The VUL uses an interest return feature subject to market gains and losses.

If you are at or near the time of retirement, you may not want to subject this money to losses. To that end, let's focus our discussion on the benefits and features of the IUL.

Indexed Universal Life

The IUL can offer the potential for cash value accumulation *outside* of the stock market. Like a retirement savings vehicle, it offers tax-deferred growth, but you are funding this strategy with money you're paying taxes on. You cannot deduct these contributions come tax time, but that means you're free from the IRS rules about when and how to spend this money. There are no RMDs, and you don't have to wait until you are age 59 ½ before you spend it.

But what really makes the IUL so appealing is the indexing feature.

It's the indexing options that give you a way to accumulate funds, and it does this by *linking* the cash value of your policy to an internal index. This index seeks to mirror popular stock market indices such as the S&P 500®. This can potentially grow your cash accumulation value—and best of all, the money accumulates tax-deferred. You don't have to pay any taxes on the growth of this money, and you don't have to pay taxes when you spend it because you're going to access it as a loan. You can also use this cash value to do anything you want.

The only caveat is that because these life insurance policies take time to build, it's best to wait seven to 10 years before accessing the money so the strategy has time to go to work for you. When you get the IUL started early, you don't have to pay as much in premiums, and yet, you still get the same benefits: a policy lasting forever with growth opportunities. Most people wait to access this money as additional income in retirement.

The more you fund the policy, the more the build-up of the cash value, but it must be funded *in balance* with the death benefit. Its main prerogative is to do what good life insurance does: function as an estate planning tool that provides a tax-free death benefit to your family. But when you understand its internal benefits, that's when things can get exciting.

Please be aware that the appealing tax-free status does not apply to all IUL distributions. A loan is the only way to access the cash value tax-free. Should you simply withdraw the money—which is an option—distributions above the cost basis will be taxable. There are also other factors to consider before deciding that an IUL is the appropriate solution for you.

The IUL is most beneficial for someone who wants both a death benefit and an accumulation tool. This accumulation is linked to the stock market, so please understand that these results are not guaranteed. There are universal policies that give you a guaranteed rate of return every year— that is an option! But even when linking to the index, you can never lose money in the account due to a market drop. We can look at history to get an idea of how the S&P 500® index has performed—and over the last 30 years (1992-2021) it has averaged 9.9 percent.[56] So once again we have history but no guarantee.

Another thing to be aware of is the fee. Every life insurance company will charge fees that are factored into your policy. With the IUL, most of these fees are paid in the first 10 years. This can make the policy expensive to get out of should you change your mind.

Remember, the goal with Universal Life is to have life insurance for the rest of your life. The IUL is not a short-term commitment. If your policy is just getting started, or you lapse in your premium payments, then it may not be able to do what it was designed to do. Make sure you get good advice before getting into one of these policies. As an accumulation tool

[56] Price, Mike. Average Stock Market Return, The Motley Fool, Nov 2022, https://www.fool.com/investing/how-to-invest/stocks/average-stock-market-return/ Accessed 3/9/2023. Values do not take into consideration investment costs of any kind. Standard and Poor's 500 index (S&P 500®) is comprised of 500 stocks representing major US industrial sectors. S&P® is a registered trademark of Standard & Poor's Financial Services LLC ("S&P").

and potential source of tax-free retirement income, this can a valuable addition to your portfolio—as long as you understand the advantages and disadvantages.

Advantages:
Tax-free death benefit for your family.
Tax-deferred accumulation.
Principal protection from market fluctuations.
Interest credits that never go below zero.
Access to tax-free retirement money.
No RMDs.
Available at any age.

Disadvantages:
Requires after-tax dollars to fund.
Upfront fee structure.
A long-term time horizon of seven to 10 years.
Must be healthy to qualify.

Fast Fact: According to the U.S. Health and Human Services Department, about 70% of people turning age 65 can expect to use long-term care.[57]

LONG-TERM CARE SOLUTIONS

If you know you have a health condition, or if your spouse has a health condition, then you might already be aware of the need to plan for long-term care. Paying for this out-of-pocket can be expensive and quickly

---

[57] U.S. Department of Health and Human Services, April 2022, https://www.hhs.gov/aging/long-term-care/index.html Accessed 1/17/2023.

deplete a portfolio. A lot of people avoid doing this planning because it's unpleasant to think about, but by putting a solution in place now, before problems arise, you'll stand a better chance of getting quality care at a price you can afford.

What follows are your life insurance options for solving this problem along with a few things to consider about the advantages and disadvantages of each solution.

Traditional Long-term Care Insurance

Long-term care insurance policies help pay for the care you need if you develop a chronic medical condition. They cover the expense of hiring a professional if you'd rather stay in your own home, even if you need round-the-clock care. They can also cover longer stays in a facility if required.

But traditional long-term care insurance is expensive. The average policy in 2022 valued at $165,000 in benefits costs $950 annually for a healthy 55-year-old male and $1,500 for a healthy 55-year-old woman.[58] That's a total of $2,450 a year for a married couple. Remember, this is money you're spending on care you might never need. The costs of this insurance can also go up as you age, making it harder to stick to a predictable retirement budget.

For instance, if you're age 45 or 50 when you take out the policy, in 40 years at the average rate of inflation, you could see the cost of your monthly premiums *double*. If you're living on a fixed income, where will the additional money come from?

Age is also a factor when qualifying. According to the American Association for Long-Term Care Insurance, people over age 70 file the

---

[58] American Association for Long-Term Care Insurance 2022 Price Index for Long-Term Care Insurance, 2022, https://www.aaltci.org/news/long-term-care-insurance-association-news/2022-price-index-for-long-term-care-insurance Accessed 1/17/2023.

vast majority of long-term insurance claims—more than 95 percent.[59] While there often aren't any age restrictions, there are health restrictions, and you're more liable to rack up conditions that would prevent you from qualifying for this type of insurance the longer you procrastinate getting a solution in place.

But perhaps the biggest drawback is what we alluded to earlier: these are *use it or lose it* policies. If you need the care, great—the insurance is there. But if you don't need it, then you've paid in all those thousands of dollars for all those years with nothing to show for it but peace of mind.

If you currently have a traditional long-term care insurance policy, or you're shopping for one now, be sure to inquire about the *elimination period*.

In most cases, you won't begin receiving money from your insurance policy beginning on the day you enter a nursing home. These policies have an elimination period of 90 days where it's eliminating any insurance protection. If you're on Medicare, for example, it will typically cover the first 100 days of your nursing home stay, but each plan is different. Medicare Advantage plans usually have a co-pay every day that you're in a nursing home, starting with day one.

If you're not healthy enough to qualify for long-term care insurance, or if you *are* healthy and don't think you'll use this benefit, you might be a good candidate for a hybrid option.

Hybrid Life Insurance Options

By hybridizing a long-term care plan, you combine a long-term care policy with a life insurance policy. A hybrid policy allows you or your family to cash in at three integral moments:

---

[59] Shell, Adam. Buy Long-Term Care Insurance at the Right Age to Get the Best Value. AARP, May 2020 https://www.aarp.org/caregiving/financial-legal/info-2019/when-to-buy-long-term-care-insurance.html Accessed 1/17/2023.

1. When you're alive.
2. When you die.
3. When you need long-term care.

This option combines the benefits of life insurance with the benefits of traditional long-term care insurance. Some hybrid options even offer a return of premium (ROP) benefit where, at certain times in the contract, you can request all your money back.

Hybrid policies are also much easier to qualify for than traditional long-term care insurance. They are what's known in the business as simplified issue—which means there is no physical required, only a handful of questions.

Here's how it works:

First, you fund the policy. You can pay a single lump-sum premium or multiple payments over a certain number of years. If it turns out that you don't need the insurance, lucky you—your policy then functions similarly to a regular life insurance policy in that there's a death benefit paid to your loved ones.[60]

If, however, like so many other millions of Americans, you *do* need long-term care, your hybrid policy will pay for whatever is covered under your plan. This policy can leverage your dollar. Typically, for every $1 you put in, you'll likely get $2 or $3 back if you need long-term care. But it's your health that qualifies you, so you may want to consider this option sooner rather than later and take action before it's too late to qualify.

Usually, life insurance pays a death benefit to your beneficiaries after you die. A hybrid long-term care plan lets you use your death benefit to pay for long-term care costs, including nursing care at home, while you are still alive. Of course, this reduces the death benefit that your

---

[60] Boland, Bud, CFP®. Is Hybrid Long-Term Care Insurance Right for You? Kiplinger, Oct 2021. https://www.kiplinger.com/article/retirement/t036-c032-s014-should-you-buy-hybrid-long-term-care-insurance.html Accessed 1/17/2023.

beneficiaries would receive. For many people, this is a trade-off they are willing to make.

Annuity Riders for Long-term Care Costs

Another option for covering long-term care costs is with an annuity designed to help pay for long-term care or an annuity with a long-term care rider attached to it. An annuity is a retirement income vehicle. It gives you a regular income for a designated amount of time. Some companies have the long-term care option built into the annuity's policy, while others require the purchase of a rider, which is an add-on benefit in exchange for a small fee.

For instance, imagine you're receiving $2,000 a month in retirement income from your annuity. Should you require long-term care, either in a facility or in the comfort of your own home, the long-term care benefit would double your income, giving you $4,000 to spend as you see fit. This extra income can help you or your spouse fund the care you need the money the most. Some limitations may apply, such as the length of time the rider pays the benefits.

The exact terms of this benefit will depend on the company, but most of them will send you this money as a monthly check that you get to cash and spend as needed. The downside is that it does reduce the death benefit of the annuity because a portion of it is being paid to you while you're alive. But it can be reassuring to know that, if your health changes suddenly, you've got a source of extra cash on hand.

Fast Fact: 47% of Americans say they are more likely to buy life insurance using simplified issue, which generally means getting approval quickly and without a medical exam.[61]

HOW TO GET APPROVED

There are three ways you can be approved by the carriers for a life insurance policy, and not all types of life insurance offer all three approvals. The three ways to get approved are:
1. Guarantee issue
2. Simplified issue
3. Fully underwritten

Guarantee-issue policies are the easiest to qualify for. There is no medical exam, no health questions, and you can't be turned down. The carrier has to say yes. But not all types of insurance offer this option. The IUL, for example, does not offer guarantee-issue policies.

The disadvantages of *guarantee issue* are the higher rates and the lower death benefits. It's considered the most expensive kind of insurance in that you're paying the most amount of money for the lowest amounts of coverage, but it's beneficial if there's a health issue and this is the only way to get coverage.

Simplified issue policies are the better kind to get if fully underwritten isn't an option. You don't need to see a doctor. Simply fill out a form and answer six questions. You're on your honor to answer them honestly but be aware they do pull your medical information bureau (MIB) record.

Every time you go to the doctor, you get a credit report for your health and your MIB gets noted. With simplified issue, they look at your answers

---

[61] Scanlon, James T.; Leyes, Maggie; Fain, Mali, 2019 Insurance Barometer Study, LIMRA, March 2019. https://www.limra.com/en/research/research-abstracts-public/2019/2019-insurance-barometer-study/ Accessed 11/12/2020.

to those six questions and compare them with your MIB record. If you answered the same as what's recorded, you get approved. If there is a discrepancy, the insurance company will want clarification.

The advantages of getting approved this way are it's easy, the cost is more reasonable, and the death benefit is more generous.

Fully underwritten policies are the best ones to get if your health allows it. The more an insurance company is privy to in terms of your previous and current health, the more they can rate your risk and give you more insurance for your money.

For this option, a phlebotomist comes to your house. This person will get your height and weight and ask you to pee in a cup. If they detect elevated levels of this or that, your death benefit could be cut in half because of an issue. If you know you're not in the best of health, then you may want to consider options that *don't* require a health examination.

Regardless of the approval method, certain carriers will also have a pharmacy list. If there is a certain medication on the list that you are currently taking, that could result in denied coverage. Another odd thing the carriers look for is DUIs. If you've had one in the last two years, that may also prevent you from getting coverage, or it may mean you're paying a higher rate. All these things should be talked about and uncovered by your insurance agent before they start crowing about a low, low rate.

Fast Fact: The average cost of a funeral in 2021 was $7,848 without a casket, vault, burial plot, headstone, flowers, or obituary. [62]

---

[62] National Funeral Directors Association, November 2021, https://nfda.org/news/media-center/nfda-news-releases/id/6182/2021-nfda-general-price-list-study-shows-funeral-costs-not-rising-as-fast-as-rate-of-inflation Accessed 1/17/2023.

LEGACY WITHOUT STRESS

There are a lot of cool things you can do with life insurance that are beneficial for retired folks. One thing that comes up a lot for people is Medicaid spend down. So, let's talk about what it is and how to use life insurance to keep more of your estate intact.

What is Medicaid Spend Down?

Medicaid is a joint federal and state program that assists people with healthcare costs not typically covered by Medicare—namely extended nursing home stays longer than 100 days. There are income and asset limitations to qualify for Medicaid. That may require you to spend down assets you'd intended to leave for your loved one before you can qualify for assistance. This could deplete your retirement resources and shrink your legacy.[63]

Every state has its own rules about Medicaid spend down, so ask your insurance professional about the rules specific to your state. In some states, they *can* go after the cash value accounts in life insurance policies. So, if you or someone you love goes into a nursing home, the state will look at those life insurance policies and calculate how much money you have access to. You'll be required to spend this money *first* to pay for nursing home costs even if you intended to leave it to your family. This can make it difficult to fund final burial costs.

What is an Irrevocable Funeral Trust?

A funeral **trust** is a policy earmarked for final burial expenses. It's unique in what it does because the money goes from the life insurance company directly to the funeral home. When you take out the policy,

[63] Genworth. Understanding Medicare and Medicaid. Updated Jan 2022. https://www.genworth.com/aging-and-you/finances/limits-of-medicare-medicaid.html Accessed 3/01/2023

you'll list a funeral home and a beneficiary for any funds left after expenses, but you don't have to use that exact funeral home. When your loved one passes, you can change your mind and choose any funeral home you wish.

There are no medical questions to qualify for this policy—it's guarantee issue. It also has inflationary protections. If you put $10,000 in the trust, for example, and it builds up from the interest earned, that amount earned by the policy is protected from Medicaid spend down as well as the original $10,000.

With a funeral trust, a certain amount of money in these policies is exempt from Medicaid spend down—they can't touch it or the interest it earns—and any remaining balance, once the funeral expenses are paid, goes directly to the beneficiary listed. To learn more about this option, talk to your insurance agent.

What is a Final Expense or Burial Plan?

If you're not concerned about Medicaid spend down, then you might be a good candidate for a final expense or burial plan. These policies will also cover final expenses, but the money is paid directly to your loved ones.

This can be a big help in cases where the body must be transported from one state to another before the burial. This money can get to your loved one within 24 hours wherever they are, and funds can be used for anything—it doesn't have to go to the funeral home first. Your beneficiary receives the whole check to spend on the myriad of different expenses that come up, especially if the death occurred out of state or an automobile was involved.

These policies are whole-life based, they never expire, and the rates can be locked in. This makes them the perfect final expense policy. But for best results, you'll want to choose the right policy.

Look for a level death benefit with level premiums. Those numbers will never go up or down. For example, just $10 a month will give you an $8,000 death benefit, guaranteed[64]. Some companies offer an increasing premium—where the amount you *pay* every month goes up. But why would you want to do that? The death benefit doesn't normally go up even if you do have an increasing premium, so you're just spending more money for the same death benefit.

Know how to qualify:
- The majority of *Final Expense* plans are simplified issue—just answer the six questions and you're done.
- The majority of *Burial Plans* are medically underwritten.

Both plans have a lot of benefits to them with no disadvantages other than cost that come to mind. There are even inflationary options that some companies offer that have the IUL feel to them—the death benefit value can be linked to a market index to help address inflation. This builds up the death benefit until the time of your passing, at which point the money is transferred within one day, and they get the whole check to spend however they want.

Your loved ones are guaranteed to get a bill upon your passing. If they don't have their own money to pay for the funeral expenses, why not get one of these plans in place?

Fast Fact: The majority of people killed in auto accidents involve drivers aged 65 and older. [65]

---

[64] Guarantees are based on the financial strength of the issuing company.
[65] National Safety Council, May 2021, https://injuryfacts.nsc.org/motor-vehicle/road-users/older-drivers/#:~:text=NHTSA%20estimates%20that%20the%20majority.driver%20deaths%3A%204%2C233%20(59.5%25). Accessed 6/9/2022.

TO ROTH OR NOT TO ROTH: Your life insurance needs can change drastically as you approach and enter retirement. Many life insurance products are actually designed to provide you with many financial and insurance benefits while you are still alive and maintaining the policy. It is worth having your current policy(ies) analyzed, and you have nothing to lose by coming in for a policy review.

Below is a summary of the main points covered:
- Term insurance is an inexpensive way to fund a large death benefit in the event of life passing too quickly.
- A whole life policy covers a person's insurance needs for their *whole* life.
- Universal policies also last a lifetime, and they can be designed in one of two ways: 1) The UL and GUL are designed specifically to generate a greater death benefit; 2) The VUL and IUL are designed to generate a higher cash value.
- A hybrid life insurance policy combines long-term care insurance with a traditional life insurance policy.
- There are three ways to get approved for a life insurance policy: guarantee issue, simplified issue, and fully underwritten.

CHAPTER SIX

FINAL THOUGHTS
Roth or No?

""A good system shortens the road to the goal."
~ Swett Marden

Answering the question, "To Roth or not to Roth," isn't a simple *yes* or *no*. If it was, there would be a lot more clarity around the issue. But what we *do* know is that you can work with someone to figure out if a Roth conversion makes sense for you. You can create a retirement plan that looks at all the financial variables, balances them, and then shows you a path forward.

You have to consider how retirement has changed; how and where you will source the majority of your retirement income; what your tax situation is and what tax-efficient strategies make the most sense for you; and how factors like risk, Social Security, your health, and life insurance options may affect your future finances.

Whether or not you decide to convert money to a Roth account, if you don't know if what you are doing makes the most sense for your goals, you are just *hoping* you are doing the right thing. And hope is not a plan. When it comes to your hard-earned retirement savings, you need to *know* that you are making the right decisions.

STREAMLINE YOUR RETIREMENT

If you are reading this book, chances are that you have done a good job. You have worked, earned, saved, and invested. You probably have a decent amount of money saved for retirement. You have done a lifetime of work to get to where you are today. That deserves genuine congratulations. You did it!

Along the way, you may have gotten advice and services from financial professionals you trust. Most people I know have their "guy." They have a plumber, a doctor, an electrician, etc. who they trust and who is their "go to person" for the particular service they need. Chances are you have a financial guy, too. I'm not asking you to jump ship and abandon the trusting relationships you have built. But I am asking you to take a look at what you need and see if you have all of the tools to work toward your retirement goals.

Managing your retirement is about understanding how everything works together. Every financial decision you make has an impact on every other financial variable. This is especially true of income planning and tax planning. Without taking the other into consideration, what might seem like a good idea may not be what is best for your portfolio, your tax reality, or your overall income plan. If you have multiple advisers and financial professionals that aren't talking to each other and working together on the overall picture of your retirement, then you could end up with a lot of good ideas that stand alone, but don't work well together.

So, should you do a Roth conversion? Does it make sense for you? Instead of asking your CPA and your broker dealer and your banker and your insurance agent, you should ask someone who can see all aspects of your financial reality; someone who can run the numbers and who has the experience to give you a definitive answer.

If you think a Roth conversion might be right for you, give me a call. I have helped countless people weigh their options and do the math to figure out if converting their funds to a Roth account would benefit them.

Fundamental Wealth Designs
(651) 461-6151
www.fundamentalwd.com

ABOUT FUNDAMENTAL WEALTH DESIGNS

At Fundamental Wealth Designs, we put time and care into our process to give our clients the best chance at success in retirement. We are a holistic practice, focusing on helping individuals develop sound retirement strategies. If you are retired or approaching retirement, we are here to help you gain financial independence by designing a plan to fit your lifestyle.

Our Process

We start with a foundation meeting. We build relationships with our clients by getting to know them, including their career and retirement goals, so we can collectively design a solid foundation and future.

Next, we deep dive into your taxes and investments and take the temperature of your risk tolerance. By analyzing your current investments and tax position, we help uncover the **correlations**, fees, and risks of your current portfolio.

From there, we design a holistic plan that is based on *your* needs and goals. Our team will create written income plans, tax plans, and legacy plans that are specific to each person's circumstances. Then it is time to implement the plan and establish the foundation for a stable retirement—the most important step to reaching the retirement of your dreams.

ABOUT BILLY VOYLES, MBA/RICP®

Billy Voyles is the founder and President of Fundamental Wealth Designs. He has been in the financial and insurance business for over 17 years, gaining knowledge and expertise along the way. Billy holds both a BBA in marketing and an MBA in finance from Eastern Michigan University.

Billy is a licensed fiduciary and has passed securities examinations 6, 26, 63, and 65. He has also earned the Retirement Income Certified Professional (RICP) designation from the American College. Before starting his own firm, Billy spent a career advising other financial advisers. He founded Fundamental Wealth Designs to help fill a gap in what he believed was an opportunity to provide truly customized and comprehensive retirement plans.

Billy lives in Stillwater, MN, and enjoys spending time with his family—wife Lindsey and four children, Bo, Sunny, JJ, and Cody. He also likes to golf, fish, and enjoy time at the family cabin in Spooner, WI.

GLOSSARY OF TERMS

ACCOUNT VALUE RESTORATION – The break-even math that shows how much of a gain you will need to get back to where you were once your account experiences loss.

ACCUMULATION PHASE – The financial phase during your working years when you are saving and growing your assets.

ANNUITY – An insurance contract where you exchange a lump-sum payment or series of payment in return for a regular income that begins either immediately or at some future date.

BENEFICIARY – An individual entitled to collect assets as decreed by a written, legal document.

BUY-AND-HOLD STRATEGY – A passive investment strategy whereby market investments are bought and then held for a long period regardless of market fluctuations, so investors capture 100 percent of market gains and 100 percent of market loss.

CORRELATION – The relationship between two things within the realm of investing: if two things are highly correlated, they are moving in the same direction at the same time; if they are inversely correlated, they are moving in opposite directions at the same time.

COST-OF-LIVING-ADJUSTMENT (COLA) – Adjustments that give claimants of Social Security a way to keep pace with inflation and the rising price of goods and services.

COMBINED INCOME – Also known as your provisional income, the IRS defines combined income as your adjusted gross income, plus tax-exempt interest, plus half of your Social Security benefits.

DISTRIBUTION PHASE – The financial phase during your non-working years when you shift from saving to spending the assets.

DOLLAR-COST AVERAGING – An investment strategy practiced during your accumulation years where the same amount of money is invested on a regular basis regardless of market performance.

ESTATE PLANNING – The simple process of transferring your stuff to someone else, including the transfer of assets, obligations, or responsibilities.

FIDUCIARY – A professional who holds a legal or ethical relationship of trust to prudently take care of money or other assets for another person.

INCOME GAP - The difference between your retirement living expenses and the income from guaranteed sources such as pensions or Social Security.

INFLATION - The general rate at which the price of goods and services gradually rises.

INFLATION RISK - The risk that rising prices associated with the cost of goods and services could outpace the returns delivered by your investments.

IRMAA - An acronym for Medicare's Income-Related Monthly Adjustment Amount, which can charge a higher premium for Medicare Parts B and D for individuals with higher incomes.

LIQUIDITY - How quickly or easily you can convert an asset into cash.

PASSIVE STRATEGY - A long-term investment strategy for building wealth whereby savers purchase investments and hold them without seeking to profit from short-term price fluctuations or market timing.

PRESERVATION PHASE - The financial phase three to five years before retirement when you shift from a growth mindset to one of preservation of your assets.

PRINCIPAL - The base amount of money that you put into an investment.

PROBATE - The legal process by which the assets of the deceased are properly distributed, the objective being to ensure that the deceased's debts, taxes, and other valid-claims are paid out of their estate, and the assets are distributed to the intended beneficiaries.

RISK - The danger or probability of loss.

REQUIRED MINIMUM DISTRIBUTION (RMD) - The minimum amount you must withdraw from qualified retirement accounts such as a traditional IRA by April 1 following the year you reach age 73 or 75, depending on the year you were born.

ROTH IRA - Individual retirement arrangement made with income after the taxes have been paid where designated funds can grow tax-free with no taxes due on the interest earned if the rules for withdrawal are followed.

SSA - An acronym that stands for the Social Security Administration.

TACTICAL ASSET ALLOCATION STRATEGY - An active investment management strategy for the investor with a shorter timeline that involves ongoing buying and selling of market investments with the goal of capturing a lower percentage of gains in exchange for a lower percentage of loss.

TRADITIONAL IRA - An individual retirement arrangement that provides a way to set aside money for retirement using contributions that are subtracted from your income (reducing the income taxes owed) and allowed to grow tax-free until the money is withdrawn, at which point taxes are owed on both the principal and interest earned.

TRUST - A legal document that creates an entity that is separate from you designed to hold the title to assets while following a specific set of instructions for the management and distribution of those assets.

VOLATILITY - A measure of the size and frequency of the change in stock market prices.